MW00451508

Sun Yatsen

Sun Yatsen's international connections: Chinese revolutionary Sun Yatsen, right, poses with his final wife Soong Qingling on the occasion of their wedding in Tokyo, Japan in 1915.
(*Courtesy of the Library of Congress*)

David B. Gordon
Shepherd University

Sun Yatsen
Seeking a Newer China

THE LIBRARY OF WORLD BIOGRAPHY

Series Editor: Peter N. Stearns

Prentice Hall
Boston   Columbus   Indianapolis   New York   San Francisco   Upper Saddle River
Amsterdam   Cape Town   Dubai   London   Madrid   Milan   Munich   Paris   Montreal
Toronto   Delhi   Mexico City   Sao Paulo   Sydney   Hong Kong
Seoul   Singapore   Taipei   Tokyo

Editorial Director: Leah Jewell
Executive Editor: Charles Cavaliere
Editorial Assistant: Lauren Aylward
Senior Marketing Manager: Laura Lee Manley
Senior Marketing Assistant: Ashley Fallon
Manager, Visual Research: Beth Brenzel
Photo Researcher: Sheila Norman AV
Manager, Rights and Permissions: Zina Arabia
Image Permission Coordinator: Silvana Attanasio
Manager, Cover Visual Research & Permissions: Karen Sanatar
Cover Art: Bettman/CORBIS
Full-Service Project Management: Shiny Rajesh/Integra Software Services, Pvt. Ltd
Printer/Binder: Courier Companies, Inc.

This book was set in 10/12 Sabon.

Credits and acknowledgments borrowed from other sources and reproduced, with permission, in this textbook appear on appropriate page within text.

Copyright © 2010 Pearson Education, Inc., publishing as Prentice Hall, 1 Lake St., Upper Saddle River, NJ 07458. All rights reserved. Manufactured in the United States of America. This publication is protected by Copyright, and permission should be obtained from the publisher prior to any prohibited reproduction, storage in a retrieval system, or transmission in any form or by any means, electronic, mechanical, photocopying, recording, or likewise. To obtain permission(s) to use material from this work, please submit a written request to Pearson Education, Inc., Permissions Department, 1 Lake St., Upper Saddle River, NJ 07458

Library of Congress Cataloging-in-Publication Data

Gordon, David B., 1963-
  Sun Yatsen : seeking a newer China/David B. Gordon.
    p. cm.—(The library of world biography)
  Includes bibliographical references and index.
  ISBN-13: 978-0-321-33306-3 (alk. paper)
  ISBN-10: 0-321-33306-3
  1. Sun, Yat-sen, 1866-1925.   2. Presidents—China—Biography.
3. China—History—1912–1928.   I. Title.
DS777.G67 2010
951.04'1092—dc22
[B]
                                                  2009018894

10 9 8 7 6 5 4 3 2 1

Prentice Hall
is an imprint of

www.pearsonhighered.com   ISBN 13: 978-0-321-33306-3
                                 ISBN 10:   0-321-33306-3

Contents

Editor's Preface

"Biography is history seen through the prism of a person."

—LOUIS FISCHER

It is often challenging to identify the roles and experiences of individuals in world history. Larger forces predominate. Yet biography provides important access to world history. It shows how individuals helped shape the society around them. Biography also offers concrete illustrations of larger patterns in political and intellectual life, in family life, and in the economy.

The Longman Library of World Biography series seeks to capture the individuality and drama that mark human character. It deals with individuals operating in one of the main periods of world history, while also reflecting issues in the particular society around them. Here, the individual illustrates larger themes of time and place. The interplay between the personal and general is always the key to using biography in history, and world history is no exception. Always, too, there is the question of personal agency: How much do individuals, even great ones, shape their own lives and environment, and how much are they shaped by the world around them?

PETER N. STEARNS

Author's Preface

I like to define history as the story of human beings on the move.

By this standard, Sun Yatsen (1866–1925) is an excellent subject for a historical biography. Sun was ceaselessly dynamic, leading a movement among Chinese to overthrow the last traditional dynasty of China's history and replace it with a modern-style republic. When this republic became a reality, he briefly served as its president, afterward continuing to influence his country for decades to come through the political party he created, the controversial foreign assistance he accepted, and the many writings he left behind. As one of his biographers has stated, while most people fail to live up to their full potential, Sun "tried to go way beyond his."

Sun was also on the move in a more literal sense. Living before the inception of commercial air travel, he took more than a dozen long ocean voyages—not to mention innumerable shorter boat trips between countries within East and Southeast Asia. He made these trips in order to chat, plot, and plead with a tremendous variety of people worldwide. As another of his biographers has phrased it, he was the "traveling salesman of the revolution" against the Qing government—the dynasty he opposed. Among the Chinese, groups with a potential interest in overthrowing that increasingly inept government included peasants, merchants, scholars, soldiers, Christian converts, and ethnic Chinese living overseas. And Sun's contacts extended still further, to sympathizers in Japan, Europe, and the United States. This strong international dimension of Sun's activities makes his life story particularly appropriate for the Library of World Biography series.

Moreover, the very era in which Sun Yatsen lived was exceptionally filled with change, leading American author Mark Twain to characterize it as the "raging, tearing, booming nineteenth century." Twain was not exaggerating: The nineteenth century was the period in which the world as we know it today first took shape. It was the age in which industrial factories, trains, steamships, telegraphs, professional sports, bacteriological medicine, and modern advertising all helped to create a new and faster way of life. At the center of many of these changes was the steam engine, which by the nineteenth century gave enterprises that employed it huge advantages over competitors near and far.

With the benefits accruing from steam and mass production, nations like Britain, France, Germany, and the United States steadily developed modern consumer economies. And especially in the later nineteenth century, they became eager to expand their territorial control to faraway places. By expanding, they could find new sources of raw materials, establish new markets, and gain prestige at the expense of their national rivals. Historians usually call this effort at expansion "imperialism" —the pursuit of empire—and it strongly affected the entire world, including the China in which Sun Yatsen lived.

Sun's China was clearly on the receiving end of Western imperialism. It lost several wars to Western countries, and before the nineteenth century was over it lost one to its modernizing neighbor Japan as well. Sun and an increasing number of other Chinese felt that their government was incompetent to deal with the new challenges it faced. Accordingly, they aimed to overthrow that government and replace it with one that could hold its own in the modern world. This is what led Sun to abandon his initial career as a British-trained medical doctor to become China's first professional revolutionary.

To overthrow the Chinese government of his day, Sun created organizations that brought together the widely disparate groups with which he had contact. He also met with a variety of foreigners, including the very imperialists who were seeking economic advantages in his country. At whatever cost, he wanted to see China's emperor-centered government replaced with a modern republic that could lead China into a new era of prosperity.

Sun succeeded in part of this effort in 1911, the year that revolution broke out against the Qing dynasty. From this point onward, his aim was to establish a stable republic that would both spur economic growth and spread the benefits of that growth broadly among its citizens. He failed on this score: Following the 1911 revolution, China was ruled for several years by a corrupt general and then by regional warlords who typically placed their own military strength above the needs of China as a whole. Sun died in 1925 while the warlords were still in charge.

He did, however, establish a tight-knit political party called the Guomindang. With assistance from Soviet Russia, this party prepared to reunite all of China beneath a single modern government. It also temporarily allied itself with the Chinese Communist Party, which sought a still more radical transformation of China. After Sun's death, his Guomindang led a campaign to reunite China by force. Its new leader, a political conservative named Chiang Kaishek, broke violently with the Chinese Communists and established a military rule over China that was centered on himself. This led to roughly 20 years of intermittent fighting between Guomindang armies and Communist rebels within an ever-changing world context.

In 1949, the Chinese Communists were able to defeat the Guomindang and establish an especially firm rule over China. While the Guomindang withdrew to the coastal island of Taiwan, the Communists under their leader Mao Zedong led massive, sometimes disastrous, efforts to modernize China's countryside. Accordingly, China since the mid-twentieth century has been split in two: The Communist Party has ruled over China's vast mainland, while the Guomindang has almost invariably held power over Taiwan.

The unifying theme within all of this confusion has been the effort to replace China's traditional dynastic government with something better suited to the modern world. Virtually, all Chinese today regard Sun Yatsen as extremely central to this effort. Sun espoused what he called the Three People's Principles: nationalism, democracy, and people's livelihood. Both Communist and Guomindang leaders today claim to promote these principles in the way they actually govern and they never tire of crediting Sun with having guided them in the correct direction.

The life and deeds of Sun Yatsen have been subjected to intense scrutiny by Asian and Western historians alike. My understanding of his life as presented in this biography draws on this continuing academic "conversation"—the articles, books, and book reviews that take Sun as their theme—as well as on direct evidence of Sun's words and activities. Essentially, my perspective is as follows: I regard Sun as having persistently—and, often, courageously—labored to strengthen China as a whole for the challenges it would face in a modern world comprised of nation-states. At the same time, I recognize his many errors, deceptions, and personal shortcomings as underscored by Western historians. China was not always well served by the leadership he offered it. Moreover, I am well aware that Sun as a political actor was willing to sacrifice much of what is usually meant by democracy in order to achieve his nationalistic ends. I do not rashly condemn Sun's aggressive expansion of the Guomindang in the last several years of his life, however; rather, that expansion strikes me as a realistic—if sometimes extreme—response to China's chronic warlordism and limited options at the time.

All of these positions are contestable. Historians' sense of the past—an individual's, a group's, or the world's—is continually subject to reinterpretation based on new information and new frameworks for understanding that information. If I were to make different intellectual choices as to how to assess Sun's lifework, this biography would possess a different flavor and would draw the reader toward different conclusions. Please keep this in mind as you proceed through this book.

In my research on Sun Yatsen, I have encountered three major interpretative frameworks, which I can broadly distinguish as (1) mainstream Chinese, (2) Western, and (3) Western revisionist. Naturally, there are numerous variations within each of these categories and the views of many researchers reflect the influence of more than one of them. Painting with admittedly broad strokes, then, let us briefly acquaint ourselves with how these perspectives look.

Sun's sheer importance to twentieth-century Asian history has earned him the attention of a host of authors, many of them Chinese. Chinese authors have typically assumed that if Sun was widely respected at the end of his life, he must have earned such respect at an early point as the result of a principled and forthright character. Consequently, they often portray him as a born leader of men, rebuking Qing officials and foreign imperialists to their faces for their failure to do what is right for China and its people. Naturally, there is a major split within Chinese interpretations of Sun between writings in Communist China and writers in Taiwan: The former invariably present Sun as sympathetic to the Communist cause, while the latter treat his alliance with the Communists as strictly tactical. Nevertheless, the overall impression left by both sets of writers is that Sun was a respected leader with influence over large numbers of Chinese from virtually the moment he decided to seek the overthrow of the Qing dynasty.

In contrast, the principal view of Sun for decades among American and European historians of China has been based on the assumption that heroes usually have feet of clay. As a result, Western biographers, notably Harold Z. Schiffrin, Marius B. Jansen, C. Martin Wilbur, and Marie-Claire Bergère, have sought to debunk the idealized images prevailing in Chinese sources. Sun in their depictions appears to have been far less influential—and far less sensible—than most Chinese authors have claimed. Indeed, their image of him stresses desperation and deceit: Sun, they contend, outlandishly exaggerated his power to a wide range of interlocutors in the hopes of attracting their support to his cause. In a similar vein, they highlight Sun's self-abasing offers to representatives of foreign governments as a counterpoint to his public identification with Chinese pride. In short, Sun comes across in many Western biographies primarily as a hustler rather than as the dignified statesman that Chinese biographers have presented him as being.

During the past decade, a new revisionist trend has emerged in Western historiography on Sun, and as one might expect, it is based on new assumptions. This trend is principally associated with historians John Fitzgerald, Michael Tsin, and Michael G. Murdock. It appears not in biographies of Sun but in academic studies of the rise of the Guomindang in the 1920s—a story in which Sun plays a central role. The new assumption that these authors bring to their subject is that modern nationalism is a primarily negative force that manipulates individuals and communities into committing their energies to unnecessary national purposes. This assumption leads the authors to a view of Sun that departs from both the mainstream Chinese perspective *and* the earlier assessment of Western biographers. In contrast to the dominant Chinese perspective, the new approach does not celebrate Sun for his contributions to Chinese nationalism; on the contrary, it censures him for these contributions. Moreover, in contrast to earlier Western biographical assessments, the new approach does not disparage Sun for having pretended to possess far more power than he actually did; rather, it criticizes him for having extended the power of his party—the Guomindang—all too adeptly. Most importantly, the approach takes Sun to task for having restructured his mid-1920s government in the city of Guangzhou as a "party state" —a government and (he hoped) nation entirely identified with a single political party. In place of earlier images of Sun as commendable or foolish, this reading presents him as frighteningly shrewd.

As we have seen, my outlook on Sun Yatsen draws on all three of these interpretive tendencies: As an individual he was complex enough to be principled or craven, ardent or calculating, depending on the circumstances he faced. At heart, however, my interest in Sun lies less in judging him—stamping him as a hero or a villain—than in utilizing his life story to explore the fascinating, complicated world he faced. Indeed, I have written this book primarily for use in world history courses, where Asian history is sometimes neglected owing to the tight schedule under which such courses operate. Accordingly, I have accentuated Sun's international connections to facilitate the use of his story as a bridge between global trends and East Asian developments. I have also configured the first chapter of the biography to provide world history students with a brief refresher on China's overall characteristics and position within world history.

The reverse side of modern China's participation in global trends is that it has helped shape some of those trends. This is especially true today, as China rapidly transforms itself into the international powerhouse that Sun dreamed of. In this respect, Sun's life story—occurring as it did on the dividing line between traditional dynastic rule and the search for what would replace it—enables us to understand a broad swath of China's road to contemporary prominence.

A Note on Chinese Spellings

Chinese is a tone language, as English is not, with the result that it is not possible to capture completely the sound of a Chinese word by spelling it out in English letters. For example, the Chinese word *mai*, pronounced with a tone that first falls and then rises, means "buy." On the other hand, the word *mai*, pronounced with a tone that simply falls, means "sell." Short of placing a diacritical mark over each syllable, there is no way to indicate this sort of distinction alphabetically. As a result, systems of transliterating Chinese words in English should always be regarded as approximate.

The two major systems that are nevertheless used to transliterate Chinese are Wade-Giles and *pinyin*. *Pinyin*, the newer system, is the one in use in China today and it has also been adopted by most scholars and journalists worldwide. I have used *pinyin* for most of the Chinese terms, proper names, and place names that appear in this book. It is generally not very difficult, but it has a few eccentricities that the reader must be aware of. Specifically, the pinyin "c" is pronounced like *ts*, the pinyin "q" is pronounced like *ch*, the pinyin "x" is pronounced like *sh*, and the pinyin "zh" is pronounced like *j*. As an example of how this works in practice, "Qing"—as in Qing dynasty—is pronounced like "ching."

I have refrained from using *pinyin* for several terms. For example, I have spelled out two important names—"Sun Yatsen" and "Chiang Kaishek"—with the older spellings by which Americans first learned of these figures many decades ago. For better or worse, these spellings have become standard for English writing on these figures (though I follow the practice of recent writers in eliminating the hyphen that used to be placed between the first and second syllables of their personal names, e.g., "Yat-sen"). The spellings of Sun Yatsen and Chiang Kaishek, respectively, display an additional peculiarity, in that they actually represent pronunciations used in *Cantonese*, a highly distinctive dialect of Chinese utilized in southern Guangdong province. This is because the Chinese who immigrated to the United States typically came from Guangdong and nearby areas, and it was they who spread their pronunciations among other Americans.

As further exceptions to my preference for *pinyin*, I refer to several locations by names long used in the West: these include Hong Kong and Tibet. In most cases, however, I utilize *pinyin* spellings and standard Chinese pronunciations for both people and places. When in doubt regarding the pronunciation of a Chinese term that is highlighted in the text, please refer to the Glossary, where I provide rough English approximations.

Acknowledgments

The first seeds of the book you hold in your hands were planted on a trip that I took to Beijing, China, in December 2003. In Beijing, my Chinese fiancée and I paid a visit to the palatial former residence of Soong Qingling, Sun Yatsen's last wife. Within the residence, we entered a large hall that served as a museum housing artifacts from Qingling's life. I was already well aware of Sun Yatsen because my father had cowritten an academic monograph on his thought some years earlier. I knew about the glamorous Soong sisters as well, but sometimes found it difficult to keep straight in my mind which of the three of them had married which historical figure! Now, however, I was visiting a grand house that belonged to a single Soong sister, Qingling, who had married Sun early in her life and had later allied herself with the Communist cause. With this as my starting point, I was soon able to grasp the relations among the leading figures in the period.

The exhibit itself contained a number of unusual items, including a life-sized embroidery reproducing a famous photograph taken at the time of Qingling's and Sun's 1915 wedding in Tokyo, Japan. As modern Japanese history is my academic specialty, this especially piqued my interest. All in all, I grew captivated by the displays presenting Qingling's life and her linkages with Sun Yatsen, Japan, and the United States (where she received part of her education). In tandem with this, I also began to view Sun differently, as a human being with a complex life history rather than simply as a politician whose actions set the stage for other, more famous figures.

The following spring, I received a routine mailing for Pearson Longman's Library of World Biography series. Upon reading it, I decided that I would like to write a biography of Sun Yatsen for the series as a way of combining two of my strongest passions, namely, East Asian history and world history. Soon after my proposal to do this was accepted, my debts to colleagues and institutions began to accumulate.

I quickly set out to read everything I could about Sun and his world. Pearson Longman generously provided me with an advance on my projected royalties that helped defray the cost of traveling to China for further research. As a result, in December 2004, I returned to China, this time to visit sites in the Yangzi River delta associated with Sun's life and work. I have had several fine editors in the course of this project: Erika Gutierrez and Janet Lanphier at Pearson Longman and Charles Cavaliere at Pearson Prentice Hall once responsibility for the series shifted there in the wake of corporate restructuring. All have provided excellent advice and encouragement. In addition, Peter N. Stearns, academic editor for the series, has furnished suggestions along the way that were all the more effective for their haiku-like concision.

The Shepherd University Professional Development Committee generously permitted me a sabbatical leave of absence for the spring of 2007 for the purpose of completing the manuscript. This same committee also provided a substantial grant that enabled me to travel to China during the course of the sabbatical, for which I am especially grateful. On this third trip, I visited sites associated with Sun in the far-southern Pearl River delta, where Sun spent both the first and the last years of his life. With this additional experience under my belt, I completed the manuscript several short months later.

Any book is ultimately a collaborative effort. Accordingly, I owe thanks to numerous people for their assistance and encouragement as I composed this biography. My wife, Christina Lu, has contributed immeasurably to my understanding of modern China and enthusiastically supported my efforts to explore Sun and his times. I dedicate this book to her. My friend Nick Schenkel read each chapter immediately after I completed it and provided steady encouragement. Michael Austin (Newman University), another friend and a specialist in seventeenth-century English literature, made recommendations that have greatly increased the clarity of the work. My father, Leonard H. D. Gordon, generously opened his files to me and cheered on my rival effort to make sense of Sun's life story. Theresa Smith, the interlibrary loan coordinator at Shepherd University's Scarborough Library, tirelessly tracked down innumerable Sun-related books that I requested at various stages of the project. Finally, I wish to extend a hearty thanks to all of the reviewers who participated in in-house reviews of part or all of the manuscript of this book: Ling Z. Arenson (Depaul University), Jean K. Berger (University of Wisconsin-Fox Valley), Liping Bu (Alma College), Thomas D. Curran (Sacred Heart University), James Gao (University of Maryland), Andrew Goss (University of New Orleans), David Kenley (Elizabethtown College), Alan Lamm (Mount Olive College), Xi Lian (Hanover College), Paul Lococo Jr. (Leeward Community College), Paul J. Morton (Covenant College), Denis Paz (University of North Texas), Harold M. Tanner (University of North Texas), and Lisa Tran (Cal State Fullerton)

Their various suggestions and corrections have brought the text to its present level of accuracy and readability.

Naturally, I am solely responsible for any factual errors that remain in this work.

Sun Yatsen

Sun Yatsen

When there is a general change of conditions, it is as if the entire creation had changed and the whole world been altered, as if it were a new and repeated creation, a world brought into existence anew.

—IBN KHALDUN
Fourteenth-century Arab historian

1

High and Dry

The year was 1894. Sun Yatsen was a 27-year-old physician in charge of the East-West Apothecary, a bustling clinic in the southern Chinese metropolis of **Guangzhou**. However, Sun had left Guangzhou (also called Canton) and had traveled some two thousand miles because he had something beyond medical practice on his mind: He wanted to reform his country. He had arrived in the northern port city of Tianjin, where **Li Hongzhang**, the most powerful official in the Chinese government beneath the emperor, had his offices. Sun fondly imagined that Li might grant him an interview, pay him to travel to France to study ways to produce silk, and put him in charge of efforts to mechanize Chinese farming. However, it all had to start with a letter.

To attract Li's favorable attention, Sun had written a lengthy document explaining who he was, what worried him, and what he wanted to do about it. He began with who he was, that is, a native of south China who had studied abroad in his youth and had earned a British medical degree. He presented himself as someone who had been observing Western countries for a number of years, continually analyzing what made them rich and strong.

What was the secret to the success of the modern West? According to Sun, it was simply that their countries methodically used what they had: "[T]heir people can fully employ their talents, their land can be fully utilized, their natural resources can be fully tapped, and their goods can freely flow." So long as the Chinese government missed this larger picture and continued to focus narrowly on building stronger ships and more powerful guns, it was, in his words, "ignoring the root and seeking the flower." In short, China needed to change—quickly.

Sun pointed out that merchants in China faced giant obstacles. For example, they had to pay taxes on their goods every time they entered a new province— taxes that corrupt officials would raise sharply to line their own pockets. It was as though "the skies are full of storms and the ground full of thorns wherever one goes." This was especially harmful because harassing merchants prevented China from realizing its nearly limitless potential.

As Sun saw matters, commerce created national power: "In the West the interests of state and those of commerce flourish together . . . The reason why Britain can conquer India, control Southeast Asia, seize Africa, and annex Australia is because

1

of its commercial strength. National defense cannot function without money, and money for the military will not accumulate without commerce. The reason why Westerners are ready to pounce like tigers on the rest of the world and why they bully China is also due to commerce." The message is blunt: For China to survive, it will have to imitate its Western imperialist tormentors, at least to the extent of encouraging commerce rather than standing in its way.

In sum, it is clear what was worrying Sun: His own country was weak, while savvy, aggressive Western countries were strong. Commerce was the solution, but commerce could not flourish in isolation. It needed government support—in the form of not only fewer taxes on merchants, but also more machines for producing goods and more railroads for moving those goods around quickly and efficiently. There was plenty of work to be done, and the starting point had to be agriculture, the heart of the Chinese economy.

Sun recommended himself as the best person to lead the effort to emulate the West in agriculture. Such an effort would require not only the diffusion of farm machinery but the establishment of numerous agricultural schools—including

A photo of Li Hongzhang, the official to whom Sun wrote his 1894 letter, in the 1870s. (© *CORBIS All rights Reserved*)

a special school to train the teachers who would teach at all of the *other* agricultural schools. Sun was confident, however, that he could help Li Hongzhang assist China to become the rich, strong nation it deserved to be.

Sun gave the letter to one of Li's secretaries. Li never provided a response, leaving Sun to return home to Guangzhou, high and dry.

The Rome of the East

A good way to begin thinking about Sun's country is to regard it as the Rome that never fell. Two thousand years ago, there were two gigantic empires in Eurasia: Rome on the west end and China on the east end. The two empires were similar in striking ways: Each had roughly 50,000,000 inhabitants, a vast network of roads, and predatory nomads living to its north. In roughly AD 500, Rome split in two and its western half splintered further into the innumerable rural plantations of which it was comprised. Later generations of Europeans dreamed of re-creating the political unity that Rome had achieved, but no one ever succeeded at the task for more than a brief period. In contrast, whenever China fractured—as it did, chaotically, every few hundred years—it invariably came back together under a new dynasty.

In short, China had staying power. It also had antiquity: China was one of the earliest centers of human civilization on earth. If we define civilization broadly as farms and cities, China certainly possessed it by 2000 BC—if not earlier. The farms and the cities first appeared in the expansive Yellow River valley, where northern China is located today. If the thrust of modern American history has been westward, with pioneer settlement moving from the east coast to the Mississippi River and beyond, the thrust of Chinese history has been *southward*, with settlement moving from the Yellow River down to the Yangzi River and on to the semitropics of the far south.

Northern China—centered on the Yellow River—and southern China—centered on the Yangzi—are very different places. While the north is a vast, dry plain dominated by wheat farming, the south is wet, mountainous country covered with irrigated rice patties. Over time, stereotypes emerged within China regarding how people in the two areas think and act. Northerners, the stereotypes held, were prairie folk—strong, silent, and slightly obtuse—while Southerners were shrewd traders—smart, talkative, and perhaps less than fully trustworthy. Sun grew up in the far south, and during his lifetime many Chinese viewed him through the prism of the "city slicker" image that they held of his region.

Despite the deep division between north and south, China saw itself as a unified civilization. More boldly, it regarded itself as the center of *world* civilization. The Chinese word for China, *zhongguo*, expresses this self-image: The first character *zhong* simply means "center," while the second character *guo* means "country." In combination, the meaning of these characters becomes "country at the center (of the world)." While other ancient civilizations such as Egypt held similar views of themselves, no one else has maintained it so doggedly for so long. Given such a national self-image, it was especially painful for Chinese like Sun Yatsen to have to argue that China needed to abandon many of its traditions in order to stay afloat in the modern world.

The Confucian Heritage

What lay at the base of the long-accepted claim that Chinese civilization was uniquely central? It was the notion that China had developed an ideal pattern of social life that was rooted in family roles. While the roles themselves had existed since virtually the beginning of Chinese civilization, it was Confucius who first built an explicit philosophy around them in roughly 500 BC. According to Confucius, being a good person consists of adhering to one's various social roles. Such roles, he held, came in pairs, as for example, father/son, husband/wife, and ruler/subject. In each of these cases, the social superior—the first-named in the above pairs—owed kindly guidance to their inferior, while the inferior—the second-named in the pairs—owed obedience and gratitude in return. Confucius held that the observance of detailed rules associated with the roles would reduce anarchy and increase order and respect throughout society.

Politically, the figure at the apex of Chinese life from roughly 200 BC onward was the emperor. Indeed, later generations of Confucianists saw his role as uniquely important: As China's supreme leader, he had to provide the ultimate ethical example for everyone in China and beyond. So long as the emperor performed this role adequately, they held, heaven would favor him with a rich and strong country. As emperors increasingly departed from ethical norms, however, heaven would signal its displeasure by sending down floods, famines, and other disasters. If, at this point, someone raised an army to overthrow an evil emperor and succeeded in setting themselves up in his place, the very success of their effort revealed that heaven had handed its mandate over to the new emperor and his descendants. One way or another, the Confucianists held, heaven would eventually nudge China back to its ethical center of gravity.

Beneath the emperor, a class of officials staffed the government bureaucracy at the national, provincial, and district capitals. Anyone who sought to join the bureaucracy had to be able, first, to read and write the Chinese language, which is written with several thousand (!) ideographs. Beyond mere literacy, however, prospective officials also had to pass grueling written exams regarding classic Confucian texts. Men who managed to pass even the lowest level of exams—possible only after years of intense study—regarded themselves as a breed apart from ordinary Chinese. While literate, Sun Yatsen had never passed, taken, or studied for the exams. In a country dominated by intelligent, snobbish "gentry," Sun's lack of Confucian scholarly background would often haunt him, driving him to work still harder toward his goals.

Manchu Rule

By the time Sun was born, China had seen numerous dynasties—some spectacular in their artistic and scientific achievements—rise, fall, and pass away. The dynasty in power during Sun's youth, the Qing, had begun several hundred years earlier, in the mid-seventeenth century. As it happened, the rulers of the Qing were not Chinese but were instead foreigners called

Manchus. The Manchus first emerged as the main nomads of "Manchuria," a snowy, resource-rich region north of the Great Wall. As the preceding Ming dynasty crumbled, the Manchus swept through an open gate of the Great Wall—built to keep foreigners like them *out*—and established their rule over all of China. In the eighteenth century, the Manchus went on to expand China's borders farther than any Chinese government had ever done, engulfing Mongolia, Tibet, and a large portion of Central Asia. For a time, then, they were a smashing success.

The Manchus ruled China for 267 years in all. Oddly, they owed their success to two contradictory policies: assimilation and separatism. Culturally, they assimilated themselves to the Chinese scene they had conquered. They claimed that they were the latest inheritors of heaven's mandate and that they would give China the benevolent Confucian rule that their Ming predecessors had ceased to provide. In keeping with Chinese sensibilities, they carefully left the examination system and government bureaucracy intact and offered the standard Confucian pomp at the imperial palace in **Beijing.**

Was everything business as usual, then? No: The Manchus feared that complete assimilation into China would deprive them of their privileges as foreign conquerors. They needed to stand out as well as fit in, and they adopted certain policies to that end. These policies included reserving certain government positions for themselves, avoiding intermarriage with the Chinese, and demanding that every Chinese male grow his hair in a lengthy ponytail called a queue. Through such actions the Manchus drew a metaphorical line between themselves and the Chinese, even as they drew a more physical line by garrisoning most of their kin in military bases scattered around China.

Aside from the presence of nomads-turned-Confucianists at the helm, the other major development in the early-to-middle **Qing dynasty** was that China's population was skyrocketing. Indeed, it rose from roughly one hundred million in the mid-seventeenth century to *four times* that number by the end of the nineteenth century. What drove much of the increase was new crops—corn, potatoes, and peanuts—that had entered China through the Spanish Philippines. These high-yield crops performed the same magic in China that they did elsewhere in the world: They increased the food supply and allowed the population to expand. China nevertheless turned out distinctively, as by the nineteenth century its increase in population exceeded its increase in foodstuffs, yielding less food per person. Meanwhile, China's bureaucracy possessed the same small number of officials that it did back at the beginning of the Qing dynasty. The result was that the country was growing too populous—and too poor—for its one-size-fits-all government to handle.

The Frightening Nineteenth Century

Other problems began to appear by the early nineteenth century, the most threatening being British commercial expansion. By this time in world history, Great Britain's industrial revolution was well underway and the British East India Company was absorbing widening swaths of India. While British traders in Asia were buying large quantities of tea from China, however, the Chinese were buying little in return. Moreover, the British traders had become increasingly unhappy with the Qing government's policy of confining all British commerce to the single city of Guangzhou in the far south.

The solution that British traders devised to counter the trade imbalance was to ship the narcotic opium, grown in India, into Guangzhou in exchange for tea. As eager British traders shipped in ever-larger quantities of the drug, an increasing number of Chinese—including some officials—became addicted. In the 1830s, the Qing government decided to suppress the opium trade. British traders quickly called on the British government to come to their defense, and when the latter complied, the result was the **Opium War** (1839–1842). The war was basically a series of scattered naval engagements off of China's southeast coast, leading the British with their superior battleships to a lopsided victory over the Manchu-led Qing forces.

The **Treaty of Nanjing** (1842), which Great Britain and China signed at the end of the war, opened several new ports, including Shanghai, for British trade. It also gave Britain permanent possession of the conveniently situated island of **Hong Kong**. A related treaty endowed British citizens residing in any newly opened port with the right of **extraterritoriality**, that is, the right to be tried under British rather than Chinese law should they commit any crimes. This right did not apply in reverse—Chinese citizens who committed crimes in Britain were still subject to British law—leading many Chinese to label the treaty an "unequal treaty." Similar treaties with France, Germany, and the United States soon extended the same unequal provisions to the citizens of those nations. Collectively, these treaties are essential for understanding China during the final decades of the Qing dynasty. Casting a long shadow, they remained in force throughout Sun Yatsen's life and were still in place when he died in 1925.

China in the middle of the nineteenth century faced internal problems that matched its external ones. In the early 1850s, a gigantic uprising known as the **Taiping Rebellion** materialized in southern China under the leadership of one Hong Xiuquan. Hong, influenced by Christian pamphlets he had received in Guangzhou, believed that he was the younger brother of Jesus Christ, charged with a mission to remove the unjust, ungodly Qing dynasty from Chinese soil. With the help of several military geniuses, his movement fought guerrilla battles that brought virtually all of south China under his control. The uprising gradually lost steam after it established the city of Nanjing in the Yangzi delta as its capital. While it lasted, however, the Taiping Rebellion affected every province of China and devastated several fertile provinces located near the delta. Its human toll was particularly horrific: Over the 13 years of the uprising, an estimated twenty million people died in the incessant fighting between the rebels and the government. Tragically, this would render it the bloodiest war in *world* history prior to World War II in the twentieth century.

Powerful Western nations like Britain and France chose to support the Qing government over the eccentric Taiping rebels. This did not prevent them from militarily attacking the Qing government during the uprising, however. The British government was especially upset that the Qing emperor would not receive

Map 1: China and its neighbors, with present-day boundary markings
(*Adapted from A Brief History of the Human Race New York by Michael
Cook, W.W. Norton, 2003, page 178.*)

British emissaries as his equals and fought a second war, this one in north China
in the late 1850s, to compel the Qing government to change its approach. This
time the outcome was that British troops burned down the emperor's Summer
Palace near Beijing and compelled the Qing government to enforce treaties that
gave Western nations a variety of new privileges, such as the freedom to promote
Christianity nationwide in the teeth of rural gentry opposition. China, a proud
country that had long enjoyed the genuine admiration of many of its neighbors,
was gradually losing its sovereignty to aggressive outsiders.

As Sun doubtless felt after Li Hongzhang failed to acknowledge his letter of
reformist proposals in 1894, so China—or at least its educated elite—felt after
the alarming events of the mid-nineteenth century. In both cases, nothing was
proceeding as it should have been. Sun Yatsen and Qing China, respectively, were
left high and dry.

2

A Marginal Youth

Sun Yatsen was born on November 12, 1866, in the hardscrabble village of **Cuiheng** in south China. He was not born as "Sun Yatsen," however. Rather, as a child he was called "Sun Wen," with *Sun* being his family name and *Wen* being his given name. In China, as elsewhere in East Asia, family names come first. Indeed, the issues regarding Sun's names are still more complex. After he converted to Christianity at age 18, he received the name "Sun Yixian" from a Chinese pastor. In Cantonese, the dialect of Chinese spoken in the area where Sun grew up, the pronunciation of the characters for this name comes out as "Sun Yatsen," the name by which he is known in the West.

There is one other point worth raising about what Sun is called: Most Chinese almost always refer to him by yet another name, "Sun Zhongshan." Zhongshan was an alias that he used later in his life, beginning with his first stay in neighboring Japan. It literally means "central mountain," and many Chinese take it to refer to the consistency of purpose that Sun displayed in his adult life. For the sake of clarity, I will use "Yatsen" in this book, but it is important to keep in mind that most speakers of Chinese are unfamiliar with it.

Growing Up Marginal

Sun's home village, Cuiheng, is located roughly 40 miles north of the city of Macao, then a Portuguese colony. Sun's father, Dacheng, owned a very small piece of land in Cuiheng, supplementing the income he derived from it with occasional work in Macao. As this pattern suggests, Cuiheng was no isolated rural village, instead opening at its edges to a much broader world. This openness was a product of geography: One of China's great rivers, the Pearl, forms a wide delta in the region as it flows into the Pacific Ocean. The city of Guangzhou (Canton) lies within this delta approximately 60 miles north of Sun's village, while the city of Hong Kong lies approximately 60 miles east of the village. All of these cities, in their turns, provided immigrants to growing communities of Chinese living overseas. Clearly, the stretch of coastal China in which Sun lived as a boy faced outward through webs of relationships that spread continuously beyond China itself.

Map 2: The Pearl River Delta (*Adapted from Sun Yatsen by Marie-Claire Bergere, Stanford UP, 1998, page 94.*)

Not much is known about Sun as a child: His family, after all, was poor and ordinary, and few records remain. The family's poverty meant that it could not afford to keep Sun in school consistently. Nevertheless, he was able to learn basic reading skills at the local elementary school and to become familiar with the Confucian classics by memorizing standard passages from them.

One other piece of information that we know about Sun as a child is that at the age of 10 he learned about the Taiping Rebellion from an uncle who had participated in it as a rebel. The Taiping Rebellion took place primarily in south China, and even after the government crushed the rebellion, anti-Manchu sentiment remained strong in the region. Sharing this mind-set, Sun would admire the Taiping rebels, and particularly their leader Hong Xiuquan, throughout the rest of his life.

Sun's only sibling was a brother, **Sun Mei**, who was 12 years his senior. In 1871, at the age of 17, Sun Mei decided to escape his family's poverty by immigrating to the Hawaiian Islands in the mid-Pacific. Starting as a hired agricultural laborer, he saved enough money to open a store, and later, to manage his own rice plantation and cattle ranch. Nicknamed the "king of Maui"—his adoptive island—he sent large sums of money home to his family and wrote letters that painted a rosy picture of Hawaii as a prosperous land with a liberal government. Sun grew increasingly enchanted.

Sun Mei had immigrated to Hawaii during a period of rapid change: While the islands still comprised an independent kingdom during his early years there, American sugar plantation owners overthrew the native government in 1893, paving the way for annexation to the United States. Within this murky political situation, some Chinese like Sun Mei managed through hard work and sheer luck to do far better than their families back in China. Such Chinese exemplified a rising wave of emigration to escape the deteriorating conditions in late Qing China. The bulk of these emigrants moved to nearby Southeast Asia—a source of future support for Sun's revolutionary endeavors. Others, however, traveled east across the Pacific Ocean. Overall, a high proportion of the emigrants came from Guangdong, the province where Sun and his family lived. With their shared dialect and customs, they swiftly formed tight-knit social and business networks to thrive in their new and highly alien environments.

When Sun was 13 years old, he leapt at the chance to join his brother in Hawaii. Following a brief stint at his brother's shop, he began his second education, this one entirely in English. In the absence of schools with Chinese curricula, Sun attended Iolani—a missionary school run by British Anglicans. He also began without any knowledge of the English language! Despite this, after three years of attendance at Iolani, he had mastered the language to the point of winning second prize for English grammar at the school's graduation ceremony.

One of the most important aspects of life at Iolani School was regular church attendance. Like English, Christianity was unfamiliar to Sun at the start, but he gradually began to feel its attraction. Shortly after his graduation from Iolani, he entered Oahu College—the premier educational institution in Hawaii at the time and another religious school.* In response to this sustained exposure to Christianity, Sun decided to convert, thereby provoking a confrontation with Sun Mei. Sun Mei was funding his brother's studies and both he and his father felt that conversion would amount to a rejection of his familial and cultural traditions. Indeed, Sun's father demanded that Sun return home so that he could "take this Jesus nonsense out of him." This was easier said than done: When Sun arrived at Cuiheng, he and a childhood friend, **Lu Haodong**, deliberately broke wooden fingers off of several village religious icons to show their nonbelief. The village responded by expelling the two youths. Unfazed, Sun proceeded to attend two schools in nearby Hong Kong in quick succession. At the second school, Sun was baptized by an American Congregationalist missionary, receiving the name "Yatsen," by which he is known in the English-speaking world.

Despite Sun's religious rebellion, he obediently married the woman whom his parents had selected for him: **Lu Muzhen**, a merchant's daughter with traditional values. The wedding was held in Cuiheng, to which Sun could now return. Following the wedding, Lu remained in Cuiheng with Sun's parents, while Sun himself left for further studies in Hong Kong and beyond. People in Sun's time and place did not regard such behavior as callous; the main purpose of marriage, after all, was to carry on the family line rather than to experience romantic love.

---

*American President Barack Obama attended this same institution, renamed Punahou School, as his high school nearly a hundred years later.

The earliest known photo of Sun Yatsen, taken in
Hong Kong when he was 17. *(Courtesy of the
Library of Congress)*

Sun Mei remained angry over Sun's conversion. He insisted that Sun return to
Hawaii, scolding him and cutting off his financial assistance when he arrived. These
actions had little effect, however, as Sun simply stayed with Chinese Christian
friends in Honolulu, receiving assistance from them to return to Hong Kong. In the
face of such determination, Sun Mei finally yielded. Indeed, from this point onward,
he would serve as a crucial source of money for his impetuous younger brother's
activities, travels, and family support.

Even with his funding back in place, Sun remained at the end of his teenage
rope: He needed a career. The primary options available were farming (exhaust-
ing), the military (unwelcoming to peasants' sons), and medicine. Medicine held
the greatest appeal, in part because Chinese culture respected doctors and in part
because the study of medicine opened the door to various Western sciences.
Accordingly, he entered the Canton Medical School in Guangzhou. This school
provided him with the opportunity to meet **Zheng Shiliang,** a Christian convert
and member of a large southern Chinese **secret society** called the Triads.

Sun's friendship with Zheng aroused his interest in the revolutionary potential of
the secret societies. Secret societies were organizations with elaborate initiations
whose members became sworn "brothers" to each other. Especially popular in

southern China, they appealed mainly to individuals who for one reason or another lacked family and descendants. In a Confucian society, where family was virtually everything, the lack of a family created a great psychological void. The secret society filled that void for its members by providing a substitute family and lineage. For members whose lack of family meant a lack of money, it could provide loans as well. Secret societies tended to function as social safety valves, insofar as they focused the efforts of the poor on advancement through cooperation. They had an edge, however: A number of secret societies possessed traditions of having opposed the Manchu takeover of China back in the seventeenth century. Despite the passage of so much time, many of them still dreamed of restoring the earlier Ming dynasty. Under most circumstances, the secret societies focused on innocuous everyday objectives. However, when aroused to fight—as during the Taiping Rebellion, which they joined—their tight organization and spirit of solidarity rendered them virtually invulnerable to government attempts at suppression.

Secret societies would play a central role in Sun's later revolutionary activities. Zheng Shiliang's significance lay in the fact that he broadened Sun's range of contacts to include secret societies if and when he would need them.

Sun Becomes a Doctor

After Sun attended the Canton Medical School for a year, he transferred to a prestigious new school in Hong Kong called the College of Medicine for Chinese. Sun, now 21, spent his next five years, 1887–1892, studying there. These years proved crucial to his development as a young man who alternately dreamed of establishing a secure position within society and of transforming that society to empower it in a turbulent modern world.

The founder of the College of Medicine for Chinese was Dr. Ho Kai, an early model for Sun. Ho Kai, a Westernized Chinese who had studied law and medicine in Great Britain, maintained close relations with Hong Kong's ruling British elite. While Sun attended the college, its dean was Sir **James Cantlie**, a well-connected doctor and missionary who would play a critical role in Sun's future. One of its main patrons was Li Hongzhang, the Qing official to whom Sun would eventually write his plea for wide-ranging reform. For a smart, ambitious young man like Sun Yatsen, the college was a good place to be.

It was especially fitting that the school was located in Hong Kong, then a cultural midpoint between Qing China and Victorian Britain. Until British opium traders arrived early in the nineteenth century, Hong Kong had been an obscure, rocky island possessing roughly four thousand Chinese inhabitants. Following the Opium War, however, the Treaty of Nanjing transferred control over the island to the British government. Within a few years, the colony began to flourish economically with the help of its protected deepwater harbor and a flood of refugees from the Taiping Rebellion. In keeping with its growing importance, Hong Kong's British administration built up the city in a style recognizable from elsewhere in the empire: a bustling commercial waterfront, wide streets with gas lighting, luxury villas situated on well-planted hillsides, and so on. This gave Chinese like Sun an opportunity to see up close how the modern West looked and worked.

Sun's education at the college proceeded with few difficulties, and at the end of five years he graduated at the top of his incoming class. There was a stumbling block, however: The college's curriculum did not fully comply with British standards, with the result that British authorities in Hong Kong and elsewhere would not recognize its diplomas. Accordingly, Sun's postcollege professional status in Hong Kong was identical to that of a traditional Chinese herbalist. Disappointed, Sun moved to Macao. He opened an apothecary there that combined Western and herbal medicine, only to endure a similar humiliation: Portuguese authorities compelled him to close his practice, as he lacked a Portuguese medical degree. Undaunted, he moved on to the third major city of the region, Guangzhou, where he began the "East-West Apothecary" mentioned in Chapter 1. This shop did well and opened a second branch. Praised in glowing newspaper testimonials for his skill and bedside manner, Sun briefly appeared to have found his calling as a Western-style surgeon who dabbled in Chinese herbal remedies on the side.

It is worth taking stock of Sun's situation at this time. The single greatest theme that we have witnessed throughout Sun's youth and educational training is that of *marginality.* His village upbringing, minimal schooling in the Chinese classics, adolescence in Hawaii, conversion to Christianity, and friendship with a secret society figure all highlight his distance from mainstream upper-class Chinese society during the late Qing period. On the other side of the equation, Sun also found himself stranded in the European colonial context as a highly educated Chinese whose professional credentials never quite passed muster. Psychologically, this position of betwixt and between was difficult to maintain. It was also broadly similar to that of numerous modern nationalists across the globe, whose ranks Sun would soon join as a Chinese revolutionary.

The Failure of Self-Strengthening

Sun Yatsen's letter to Qing official Li Hongzhang in 1894 would argue passionately for the modernization of virtually all areas of Chinese life. Sun certainly addressed this appeal to the right person: Li was the torchbearer for late-nineteenth-century China's attempts to develop an array of modern industries alongside its traditional ones. These attempts, taken collectively, comprise what historians call the **Self-Strengthening Movement.**

As with many other aspects of late-nineteenth-century China, the roots of the Self-Strengthening Movement trace back to the Taiping Rebellion. After initial attempts to subdue the rebellion failed, the Qing government permitted ethnic Chinese governors in affected regions to establish their own province-based armies and send them into battle against the rebels. These armies and separate anti-Taiping Western armies proved highly effective, persuading the Qing government that it needed to strengthen itself militarily in order to hold its own against foes at home and abroad. When the Taipings were defeated in the mid-1860s, ethnic Chinese leaders of the new regional armies—including Li Hongzhang—were well placed to lead modernization efforts within the government. At first, they focused mainly on military goals, such as the construction of a modern arsenal and a naval shipyard along China's seacoast.

During the 1870s and 1880s, their range of initiatives broadened appreciably to include profitable enterprises in mining, railway construction, telegraphy, and textiles. Throughout, the overall philosophy behind the movement would remain, as expressed by Chinese governor Zhang Zhidong, "Western learning for techniques, Chinese learning for the essence." As this motto indicates, the entire effort aimed finally to preserve tradition, much like concurrent attempts at defensive modernization in Japan, Siam, and the Ottoman Empire.

Unfortunately for China, its Self-Strengthening Movement emerged in a markedly unfavorable political context. The real leader of China through much of the latter half of the nineteenth-century was the **Empress Dowager Cixi**, who served as regent for two successive emperors from within her family. Cixi was not the rigid conservative that many historians have portrayed her as being. However, her government contained a number of conservative Confucianists who opposed all forms of modernization as contrary to precedent. Given the political strength of this group, Cixi felt that it was wiser for her to play the conservatives and the Self-Strengtheners off against each other than it was for her to identify herself fully with either side. This assessment led her to take a cautious approach toward the entire movement.

The result was that the Qing government—its vaunted six ministries—continued to operate as before, ignoring the new enterprises that a few provincial governors managed on the side. Moreover, the path of advancement for ambitious young men in the late nineteenth century remained that of success at Confucian civil service examinations. Inasmuch as the government did not throw its weight behind the new enterprises, they existed in an effectual vacuum despite their achievements. As historian Immanuel Hsü has stated, the era of Self-Strengthening failed to bring about the true revitalization of the Qing dynasty, serving instead as its "Indian Summer."

Just how inadequate China's self-strengthening had been was displayed in the Sino-French War, a conflict that strongly affected Sun Yatsen. Traditionally, most countries adjoining China became its tributary states by paying obeisance to its emperor and allowing him overall control of their foreign relations. Indeed, two of China's neighbors, Annam and Korea, went to great lengths to maintain this subordinate-yet-protected relationship. For Annam, however, this arrangement was threatened when France turned neighboring Cochin China (today's southern Vietnam) into a French colony. In the early 1880s, the French colonial government launched a war of expansion aimed at Annam (central Vietnam) and Tonkin (northern Vietnam). This provoked a conflict with China, Annam's traditional protector, that China had no chance of winning. In the major battle of the war, a French flotilla sailed to the only modern shipyard on China's southeast coast and largely destroyed it within a single hour of fighting. Thereafter, France amalgamated Cochin China, Annam, and Tonkin as "Indochina," a colony it maintained through the first half of the twentieth century.

In an autobiographical sketch written in his later years, Sun declared that "my decision to overthrow the Manchu regime and to establish a republic was made in the year 1885 when the Sino–French War took place." Much closer to the time of the war, he stated that he was strongly impressed by the patriotism of Chinese dockworkers in Hong Kong, who refused to service a French vessel on its way back to Southeast Asia after having bombed the Chinese shipyard. It is doubtful whether Sun genuinely became a convinced revolutionary at the time of the Sino-French War, particularly since he wrote his letter seeking a position with Li Hongzhang nearly a decade later. Nevertheless, the war was a warning bell in the night: Despite the Self-Strengtheners' best efforts, China's technological progress was nowhere near fast enough for it to defend itself effectively against hostile outsiders.

Sun and China at the Crossroads

We have watched Sun spend most of the 1880s and early 1890s as a student, first in Hawaii and then in medical schools in Guangzhou and Hong Kong, respectively. It was in Guangzhou that Sun met Zheng Shiliang, his Christian friend with contacts in the Triad Society. In Hong Kong, he made more friends, such as Chen Shaobai, another Christian and an especially bright student. Sun, Chen, and two other young men were known to spend hours together discussing politics from an anti-Manchu perspective, leading outsiders to label them the "Four Great Bandits."

Historians often ask whether Sun was a reformist or a revolutionary during his years in Hong Kong. There is evidence in both directions. On the one hand, Sun sometimes experimented with explosives at his college's chemistry laboratory, suggesting that violent revolution was on his mind. On the other hand, toward the end of his stay he wrote letters of a reformist tenor to a Qing court official with international experience and a liberal-minded businessman from his home district. Overall, his thinking remained in flux, as he later admitted: "In Western studies I was most fascinated by the way of Darwin. As for religion, I worshiped Jesus, and, as for men, I revered China's Kings Tang and Wu and America's George Washington." He was also reading numerous European authors, including Rousseau, Mill, Huxley, Marx, and Russian anarchist Peter Kropotkin. Regrettably, Sun did not write down his initial responses to these thinkers in letters, essays, or diaries. We know enough, however, to see in him the profile of a driven young man who had not yet found his life's mission.

It was Sun's friend Chen Shaobai who came the closest to witnessing the moment of Sun's transformation. In late 1893 or early 1894, Chen received a letter from the East-West Apothecary, Sun's shop in Guangzhou, informing him that no one at the store had seen Sun for days! Chen set out for Guangzhou to ascertain what had happened. Before long Sun appeared with a stack of papers— the draft of his letter to Li Hongzhang, which he had been preparing instead of attending to his business. From this time forward, Sun lost interest in his apothecary, leaving Chen to settle his affairs for him while he prepared to make the trek northward to Li Hongzhang's office in Tianjin.

In February 1894, Sun left Guangzhou together with his childhood friend Lu Haodong. Sun and Lu stopped in Shanghai, where they met fellow reformists who, like them, desired a broader and more intense version of the Self-Strengthening Movement. They also collected letters of introduction for visiting Li in Tianjin.

Sun's own letter, personally delivered at Li's office, ably summarizes the major themes of the reformists. Politically speaking, the reformists supported the Qing government. Economically, however, they saw China as a habitual low-achiever, arguing that nothing could unlock its vast potential until its government encouraged the free-flow of people to suitable jobs and of goods to suitable markets. As Sun pointed out, a better future awaited, if only China would grasp it: "When man's boundless creativity is set free and can be directed toward elucidating the endless mysteries of the universe, how can anyone be isolated or ignorant?"

Li Hongzhang already had people on his staff who had received training abroad and who held reformist views. Why then did he not accede to Sun's request that Li send him to France to study sericulture? The answer probably lies in who Sun *was*: rather than being a respected Confucian scholar with a veneer of Western expertise, Sun was a product of coastal China, that is, of a marginal environment that fused East and West in the relentless pursuit of business opportunities. As Sun biographer Harold Schiffrin declares, for elite reformers Sun "would always be merely an ex-peasant with a foreign diploma." Such a figure could never impress them.

Sun Yatsen's letter marked a watershed in his life. When Li failed to respond to it, his future path became clear: to reject the government that had rejected his offer of his services. From this time forward, he became a revolutionary, organizing a dazzling array of contacts with the aim of overthrowing the Qing dynasty.

The Sino-Japanese War

Aside from his low social status, there appears to have been a second factor in Sun's failure to attract Li's attention: especially poor timing. Sun brought his letter to Li's office just as the specter of war was appearing between China and Japan over the future of Korea. If there was to be war between these two countries, Li, as the commander of China's northern navy and the nation's foremost diplomat, would have to play a central role in it.

For hundreds of years, Korea had been the lynchpin of China's tributary system. In the later decades of the nineteenth century, however, this relationship had begun to unravel, as other foreign countries and particularly a rising Japan developed their own relations with the country. Facing these trends, Li wobbled unpredictably between treating Korea as an exclusive Chinese colony and encouraging it to pursue relations with Western powers to offset Japanese gains.

The Japanese government had long displayed an interest in Korea and had often sparred diplomatically with China over its objectives there. In 1894, an unprecedentedly large peasant rebellion broke out in Korea, prompting both Japan and China to pose as the Korean government's protector by dispatching their troops. Although the rebellion was rapidly suppressed, Japanese troops in Korea soon attacked Chinese forces, commencing the Sino-Japanese War.

This war resulted in a lopsided victory for Japan both on land and at sea. Indeed, within months Japanese troops were massed at the terminal eastern gate of the Great Wall with little standing between them and the Chinese capital at Beijing! Although Japan's military decided not to push its advantage, its success had overturned the Chinese and Western assumption that China's superior troop strength would overwhelm anything Japan could muster. Clearly, Japan's military had modernized far more aggressively and effectively than China's had. The result was the humiliating Treaty of Shimonoseki, signed by Li for the Chinese side, which gave Japanese citizens the same extraterritorial rights as Westerners at Chinese ports and transferred the large island of Taiwan off China's southeast coast to Japanese control.

Qing China's entire situation began to appear different after its disastrous defeat in this war. For centuries, China's safest borders had been those with its two closest allies, Annam and Korea. By the mid-1890s, that safety had been ripped away. Moreover, China's latest defeat was not at the hands of a faraway Western power but was instead caused by Japan, a smaller neighbor whom most Chinese had long viewed condescendingly. For such a neighbor to beat mighty China by employing the military and industrial model of Western nations seemed nothing short of bizarre. And it provided an opening for China's first professional revolutionary, Sun Yatsen.

Reviving China by Force

The Sino-Japanese War had begun in September 1894. That same month, Sun traveled to Honolulu—his first trip there in more than a decade. With the help of his brother Sun Mei, he was able to interest roughly 20 young men—out of Honolulu's Chinese population of five thousand—in his plans for revolution in China. A number of these men resembled Sun himself: Like him, they were Christian, Western-educated professionals who hailed from the district of Xiangshan in Guangdong province. As such, they comprised a nascent elite relative to the preponderance of laborers among Honolulu's ethnic Chinese. On November 24, 1894, this group met at the house of a former classmate of Sun's to found an organization known to history as the Revive China Society.

The Society came complete with an oath, a membership fee (five dollars per person), and procedural regulations. Sun administered the oath to all new members, having them place their left hand on a Bible and raise their right hand to display their acceptance of its terms. To raise more money, the Society offered bonds at ten dollars apiece that would be redeemable for ten times their value once the revolution was complete—an unabashed appeal to members'self-interest.

In the ensuing months, two additional Hawaiian branches of the Society were opened and membership increased to roughly 120 people. What were these people agreeing to do? There is no record left of the oath that they took. It is evident, however, that they were acceding to a plan to foment a regional rebellion in the hopes of sparking a revolution against the Manchu Qing government. They would serve as the "bank" for this rebellion so that Sun could purchase arms and recruit rebels back in China. When one considers that Qing government agents lived in Honolulu and could report the names of any conspirators back to China for reprisals against family members, it is evident that those who joined were either courageous or foolhardy. They also had to be atypical, as most Hawaiian Chinese at the time continued to respect the imperial institution.

When it appeared that Japanese troops might be marching toward Beijing, Sun decided to return to China to use the situation to his advantage. He went to Hong Kong and established a new branch of the Society in February 1895. Members of the new branch included such familiar friends as Lu Haodong, Zheng Shiliang, and Chen Shaobai. They also included members of the Literary Society for the Development of Benevolence, which now merged into Sun's Revive China Society. This "literary" society was headed by Yang Quyun, a Westernized Chinese businessman born in Hong Kong. Yang's group had existed for three years and had hidden its revolutionary goals behind its Confucian-sounding name. By joining forces, Sun was able to gain access to the funds at Yang's disposal.

The oath taken by members of the Hong Kong branch has been preserved. It starkly contrasted China's weakness with the strength of Western powers, concluding with a cry for radical change: "Our descendants may become the slaves of other races! China can only be restored by assembling men of determination." Despite this rhetoric, the oath neither set forth a clear plan for China's future nor encouraged members to propagandize in Hong Kong or elsewhere. Instead, the Society placed its hopes in a single regional rebellion—to occur later in 1895—that would presumably spread like wildfire out of Guangzhou to other parts of China, topple the Qing dynasty, and provoke the creation of a new government led by the aforesaid "men of determination." The naivety for which Sun was later known appears already in this farfetched scheme.

Regardless of the flaws in the larger strategy, at a regional level Guangzhou was a good choice for a rebellion. The city had numerous Triad Society members, opium smugglers, pirates, and disgruntled government troops—all of whom might serve as mercenaries for the right price. In addition, the area maintained its festering resentment of the alien Manchus. With the money they collected, Sun and Yang were able to buy weapons and prepare their transfer to a force that would sail from Hong Kong to Guangzhou, and then break into groups to attack government offices in Guangzhou while protected by reinforcements from upriver.

The rebellion was to take place on October 26, 1895. That morning, Sun's men in Guangzhou appeared at the wharf to greet the expected boat with rebels and weapons arriving from Hong Kong. At that juncture, however, Sun received a telegraph from Yang Quyun telling him that the boat would not come until the next day. As the operation required careful timing, Sun decided to call off the uprising for the time being. He sent a telegram to this effect, but it did not reach Yang on time, and Yang sent the boat the next day as promised. When the rebels onboard reached the wharf, Guangzhou's district police were waiting for them.

Even without the delay in Hong Kong, the rebellion would have encountered problems because authorities in both Hong Kong and Guangzhou had received word from informers that something major was about to take place. On October 26, Guangzhou police raided the secret hideouts of some of the rebels and captured guns, flags, and other items. The next day, the government arrested several members of the Society, including Sun's childhood friend, Lu Haodong. Defiant to the end, Lu was tortured, placed on trial, and executed.

[Sun himself narrowly escaped capture at this time.] First, he found refuge in the home of a Chinese Christian minister in Guangzhou (it was typical of him to turn to Chinese Christians when he was in danger). Next, he arranged a hasty sedan chair ride to Macao. From Macao he traveled to Hong Kong, where he boarded the first available ship, which was headed for the city of Kobe in Japan. Thus began Sun's 16 years of exile from Chinese soil.

[The Guangzhou rebellion of 1895 brought the life of Sun Yatsen into an entirely new phase. Prior to the rebellion, he had been a successful young physician and a dabbler in Western ideologies. After the rebellion, from the standpoint of the Qing government and its loyal subjects, he was virtually a terrorist.] Indeed, six months after the rebellion, a hostile article in a Chinese newspaper in Singapore endowed him with the sinister characteristics of a traditional bandit chief, namely, red eyebrows and green eyes. Leading an armed rebellion against an established government is a serious matter in any nation and for Sun, in particular, it marked a point of no return: the Qing government regularly executed people—such as his friend Lu Haodong—for less than he had done.

It is also worth reflecting for a moment on the character of the failed Guangzhou rebellion itself, as it typified rebellions Sun would lead in the future. First of all, Sun preferred to base his rebellions beyond the reach of Qing government authorities. In the case of the Guangzhou rebellion, that base was colonial Hong Kong—his collection point for troops and weapons. Second, Sun invariably hired conspirators rather than raise his own armies. [He placed abiding—and excessive—faith in secret societies as his primary source of military muscle.] Finally, [he eagerly sought foreign support for his rebellions.] In this case, he utilized his connection with Ho Kai, founder of the College of Medicine for Chinese, to garner at least a sympathetic stance from British officials in Hong Kong. [These tendencies—choosing out-of-the-way bases, hiring insurgents, and soliciting foreign support—highlight Sun's overall belief that the only way China could change was through pressure from the margins.] As someone who had been firmly planted on the margins of Chinese life from childhood onward, such an approach naturally made visceral sense to him.

3

Kidnapped in London

The debacle in Guangzhou compelled Sun to leave China at once. As his means of escape, he sailed for neighboring Japan in the company of his close friends, Zheng Shiliang and Chen Shaobai. The three men landed in Kobe, following which Sun proceeded on to Yokohama, a growing port city near the Japanese capital. In Yokohama, he established another branch of the Revive China Society within the city's Chinatown. He also underwent a visual transformation—cutting off his queue, letting his hair grow out in front, and exchanging his Chinese robe for a European suit and tie. To complete the effect, he grew a mustache in the style of a quasi-Victorian Japanese gentleman. Henceforth, many Chinese and Japanese who met Sun mistook him at first as Japanese!

In the spring of 1896, Sun traveled on to Hawaii under an alias to visit his brother. His family, whom his actions had put in danger, safely escaped from China and was soon able to join him there. Sun was by this time the father of two children, a girl and a boy, although he played little part in raising them. Instead, his affluent brother took care of his family and paid their expenses while Sun resumed his travels to solicit funds from among Chinese living overseas.

While in Hawaii, Sun had an accidental encounter with his medical instructor, James Cantlie. Cantlie too happened to be in Hawaii in late 1896 on his return to England for retirement. Sun accosted a carriage on a street in Honolulu that contained Cantlie and his family. Cantlie, surprised, invited Sun to visit him in London and even to take an advanced medical course from him there. Sun had not planned to visit London prior to this, but he cheerfully added it to his itinerary.

After renewing his contacts with the Revive China Society's Hawaiian branches, Sun proceeded on to the continental United States for his first of many visits there. He disembarked in San Francisco and spent several weeks in the local Chinatown, trying to interest Chinese laborers there in his plans for revolution. He encountered two problems, however. First, the Chinese government had diplomatic representatives in the United States who were watching his movements and warning American Chinese to avoid contact with him. Second and more broadly, most American Chinese in San Francisco and elsewhere were politically apathetic, seeking personal success above all else. To the limited extent that they thought about Chinese politics at all, they, like the Chinese in Hawaii, respected the Qing dynasty and found Sun's call for revolution frightening.

While in San Francisco, Sun foolishly posed for a photograph in his new Western clothes. A copy of this photograph made its way to Chinese diplomats, which simplified their task of tracking his movements across the United States. Meanwhile, Sun continued to solicit funds, invariably managing to raise enough money to continue to his next destination as he traveled eastward by rail. In New York City, the Chinese community gave him the same cool reception he had received in San Francisco and other locations. From New York, he set sail for Liverpool, England, arriving there at the end of September 1896.

Kidnapped at the Chinese Legation

Sun arrived in London on October 1 and the following day he paid a visit to the Cantlies at their house on Devonshire Street. They arranged lodgings for him and he settled into a routine of touring major sites in London. He continued to visit the Cantlies almost daily and they apprised him that the Chinese Legation—the term then used for the Chinese embassy to England—was located nearby. This would obviously be a place to avoid, given the Chinese government's eagerness to execute him as the ringleader of the Guangzhou rebellion.

Sun would nevertheless wind up inside the Legation as a prisoner for 12 days, an event that brought him worldwide fame. There are various accounts as to how Sun entered the Legation and what events transpired inside. Here, I will follow Sun's own account in *Kidnapped in London*, a short, widely distributed book he wrote in English with Cantlie's assistance a month after the event. I will then cast some historical doubt on one aspect of that account.

One Sunday, October 11, 1896, at 10:30 AM, Sun was walking toward the Cantlies' residence, seeking to join the family for church. At that point, a Chinese man approached him on the street and asked him in English whether he was Chinese or Japanese. Upon learning that Sun was Chinese, the man asked him what province he came from. When he found out that Sun came from the south, he shifted to speaking in the Cantonese dialect of Chinese. A second Chinese man soon joined them and the two of them invited Sun to their lodgings for a chat. Sun was worried that he would be late to meet the Cantlies, but the men held their ground. According to Sun, "I was gradually, and in a seemingly friendly manner, led to the upper edge of the pavement, when the door of an adjacent house suddenly opened and I was half-jokingly and half-persistently compelled to enter . . ." As soon as he was inside, the door was barred to his exit.

Sun was rushed upstairs, to one room and then another. An elderly English gentleman with a white beard entered what had become Sun's domicile on the third floor of the building. This was Sir Halliday Macartney, a high-ranking employee of the Chinese government in London. Macartney told Sun, "You are now in China." He stressed that since the building was the Chinese Legation, it was Chinese and not British law that applied there. He also told Sun that the Chinese minister in the United States had telegraphed the Legation with information about Sun's journey to England and had specifically asked Macartney to arrest him. At the end of the conversation, Macartney rose, left the room, and locked the door. A second lock was soon added to the door and two guards were posted outside of it. There was no way out!

Sun was quite frightened, even as servants took adequate care of him inside his room. His fear increased further when the first man who had accosted him on the street visited him and explained that the Legation planned to ship him secretly back to China and execute him for his role in the Guangzhou rebellion. Sun had a vivid sense of what this meant. As he explained years later, his "ankles [would be] crushed in a vise and broken by a hammer, my eyelids cut off, and finally [I would] be chipped to small fragments, so that none could claim my mortal remains." Moreover, all of that would come *after* the Qing government had tortured him into naming his accomplices!

Sun made desperate attempts to escape his predicament. He threw scraps of paper, weighted with coins, out of his window with messages communicating who he was and whom passersby should contact to help him. The Legation's employees collected and removed the messages. He also appealed to one of the English servants assigned to him, George Cole, by telling him that he was being

James Cantlie, Sun's medical instructor in Hong Kong and host and rescuer in London. (*The University of Hong Kong, Dept of Surgery*)

persecuted for being Christian much like the Armenians of the Middle East were (this was an issue that the English press was just then covering extensively). Cole wavered, then agreed to help Sun escape by carrying a message to Cantlie.

After Cantlie was contacted, he began wide-ranging efforts to inform British authorities regarding the situation. In short order, he appealed to Scotland Yard (the detective department of the London police), the British Foreign Office, and a local newspaper. He also arranged to have the Legation watched since he feared that it might quickly move Sun to another location. The British government initially hesitated to become involved in any effort to rescue Sun, as it lacked actual proof that he was being detained. After it confirmed that the Legation had already contacted a local shipping line, however, it placed strong diplomatic pressure on the Legation to free its prisoner. Equally important, *The London Globe* and other newspapers splashed the whole affair across their front pages. When the Legation could no longer resist the pressure and adverse publicity, it released Sun—now a national celebrity—into freedom on October 23.

Effects of the Kidnapping

The above sequence of events had a lasting impact on Sun's subsequent fortunes as a revolutionary seeking to overthrow the Qing government. Before examining the long-term effects of the episode, however, it would be helpful to inquire, again, how Sun *really* entered the Chinese Legation in London. The issue is less clear-cut than it appears. As noted, Sun claimed in his book that he had been cajoled by two Chinese males into entering the Legation, which he had never before visited and of whose precise location he was unaware. Yet Sun later boasted to his Chinese friends like Chen Shaobai that he had entered the Legation voluntarily in order to confront the Qing government directly. This broadly squares with Macartney's newspaper account, which maintained that Sun had first entered the Legation on the previous day, Saturday, with the intent of spying on it. It also squares with Cole's later assertion that he (Cole) had been specially requested to appear at the Legation on the morning of Sun's detention—despite the fact that he ordinarily did not work on Sundays—and asked to prepare the room that became Sun's domicile.

Can the various claims be reconciled? Probably not. On the one hand, Sun's description in his book of his manner of entry into the Legation rings true. If he had really wished to blacken the name of the Legation, he could have simply concocted a frightening story about his having been abducted forcibly off the street somewhere. On the other hand, it also rings fairly true that Sun would have entered the Legation directly, given his penchant for daredevil behavior. It is at any rate difficult to believe that Sun would have remained oblivious to the location of the Legation despite his ongoing conflict with Qing government authorities. It is likely, then, that Sun had had some sort of prior contact with the Legation—which confidently expected his arrival on Sunday—whether or not he had actually entered the building previously.

Sun's manipulation of the truth—possibly to more than one audience—with regard to his manner of entry into the Chinese Legation in London highlights an important aspect of the episode for his career, namely, his uncanny ability to exploit the affair for his own advantage. During both his captivity and its journalistic recapitulation afterward, Sun showed himself to be highly skilled at thinking on his feet. He intuitively grasped how to appeal to Cole to gain his help in contacting the outside world. Moreover, after he received his freedom, he consistently presented himself to the British press as a civilized gentleman who had been ill-treated and even bodily threatened by a tyrannical Oriental government. By playing to ordinary Britons' prejudices concerning China, he encouraged them to regard China's current government as an intolerable threat to humanitarian values. An aroused British populace, he hoped, would pressure its government into supporting or at least condoning his efforts at revolution.

Certainly Sun's name had become known far and wide in Great Britain and elsewhere in the West, both as the victim of a sinister kidnapping and as the man who wrote an exciting account of the experience. An important by-product of this fame is that Sun became much better known in China as well. By kidnapping Sun thousands of miles away from China, the Qing government dramatically displayed how much it feared and hated him. In order for the government to feel this strongly about him, many Chinese thought, he must have a special capacity to cause it extensive harm. Anyone who dislikes the government, their logic continued, would do well to make contact with him as the government's mighty opponent. In this way, the Qing regime actually inflated the importance of someone who, after all, had been merely a regional rebel with limited resources. To aim at Sun and miss was to make him a good deal stronger.

The episode had still other effects. For example, it greatly inflamed Sun's already strong sense of mission. The dramatic sequence of events—captivity followed by freedom—convinced him that God had personally spared him for the task of overthrowing the Qing government and replacing it with something better. This postdetention conviction has led Sun biographer Marie-Claire Bergère to label Sun an "egoistic Christian." Whether or not this label is accurate, he definitely began at this time to identify his individual well-being with that of China and vice versa.

One circumstance that did not change after the kidnapping was British policy toward China. The British government's primary goal with respect to China was to ensure maximum opportunities for British businesspeople. As the British government felt that the Qing government, in its very weakness, provided those opportunities, it tended to look favorably upon it. At the same time, it experienced frustration with the Qing government over certain issues, such as the ongoing need to provide large bribes to Qing officials. As these frustrations were usually felt more strongly by British officials in East Asia than by those in England itself, the British officials in East Asia tended to support a harder line toward the Qing dynasty and, at times, to support Chinese antidynastic activity. This corresponds to a general pattern when European colonial powers penetrated various areas of the globe: The Europeans who pushed hardest to undermine or attack native governments were typically those who represented European interests out in the field rather than high-level government officials back in Europe. In any event, European home governments could often enforce their will, and the British government did so in the case of Sun. Despite its sympathy for Sun's personal plight, the British government continued its friendly relationship with the Qing dynasty and, to this end, maintained its prohibition on visits by Sun to British Hong Kong.

After the excitement over his detention and release subsided, Sun developed a pattern of regular study at the British Museum Library, where he read widely on politics, law, naval affairs, agriculture, engineering, and other subjects. One factor that guided this reading program—lasting more than half a year—was his sense that England and other Western countries were experiencing serious problems, such as conflicts between rich and poor, alongside their many achievements. His overall goal, expressive of both his egoism and his long-term vision, was to enable a future China to avoid the pitfalls of the industrialization that the West had undergone. Having explored these issues to his satisfaction, Sun left England and returned to Japan to resume his organizational work there.

The New Imperialism Comes to China

While Sun was accustoming himself to life as an exiled revolutionary, major military and political changes were transforming the relationship between Western nations and China. These changes, part of a broader global phenomenon that historians call the New Imperialism, directly shaped the world in which Sun would henceforth operate.

During the 1880s and 1890s, the West found itself in an overwhelmingly advantageous position vis-à-vis the rest of the earth. Its new weapons—battleships and machine guns—and means of transportation and communication—railroads and telegraphs—enabled it to impose its will on non-Western nations and extract their resources for its benefit. In addition, the West experienced heavy intramural competition, as each major power feared that if it did not immediately acquire territories in a particular region of the globe, other powers would seize them first. While the results of this mixture of power and anxiety appeared most starkly in Africa, major powers—with Great Britain invariably leading the pack—also sparred for advantage in such West Asian locales as the Ottoman Empire and Persia. In those aging empires, the powers competed for "**spheres of influence,**" that is, broad regions in which they would enjoy extensive economic privileges.

Although East Asia was slightly behind in experiencing the new wave of imperialist pressure, the storm reached it in full gale by the later 1890s. The Sino-Japanese War marked the occasion—or rather, the excuse—for this. One of the stipulations of the Treaty of Shimonoseki required the Chinese government to pay the Japanese government a huge indemnity. China lacked the means to fulfill this obligation and was reduced to borrowing the money from Western powers. As a *quid pro quo*, the powers demanded that the Chinese government give them geographically defined spheres of influence with extensive railroad, mining, and timber rights. By accepting these terms, China became financially indebted to Western countries and found itself at risk of having its territory partitioned among them.

Scholars call the sudden competition for spheres of influence in China during late 1897 and early 1898 the **scramble for concessions.** Most of the resulting spheres lay along the heavily populated east coast in such areas as northeast China adjoining Russia (Russia's sphere) and southeast China adjoining French Indonesia (France's sphere). The Chinese government's inability to resist Western pressures led Westerners to deride it, increasingly, as the "sick man of Asia," much as they scornfully described the Ottoman Empire as the "sick man of Europe."

These new developments frightened Qing dynasty officials, scholars, and examination candidates as never before. On the one hand, they deeply believed in an emperor-centered Confucianism; on the other, they realized that China faced unprecedented danger. While many of them hoped that a renewed allegiance to national self-strengthening would suffice to keep China safe, others—including the man who became Sun Yatsen's bitter political rival—experimented with the possibility that a new reading of Confucian tradition could provide China with a way out of its impasse.

Kang Youwei, Sun's eventual rival, resembled Sun in many ways. Like Sun, Kang hailed from southern Guangdong, admired the late nineteenth-century modernizing regimes of Germany and Japan, and possessed an unshakable sense of mission. Also like Sun, Kang viewed technology, institutional change, and programs for the poor as essential to China's future. These resemblances were matched by equally great contrasts. Of the latter, the most important are that Kang was born into a completely different social class—the proud scholar-gentry—and that he maintained a dogged allegiance to Confucian learning and monarchical rule throughout his life.

A Confucian child prodigy at the age of seven, Kang became enamored in his young adulthood with the Western technological and institutional accomplishments on display in Hong Kong and Shanghai. Synthesizing these trends, he developed

Confucian reformer Kang Youwei
(*Courtesy of the Library of Congress*)

Kang's disciple Liang Qichao (*Courtesy of the Library of Congress*)

a novel approach to Confucius that presented him as an institutional reformer with an evolutionary view of society. This approach, detailed in such books as *A Study of Confucius as a Reformer*, was based on innovative, if strained, readings of major works in the Confucian canon. Actually, this sort of rereading is broadly similar to what occurred in many non-Western societies in the nineteenth century: Mavericks in various lands were reinterpreting traditional systems of belief to sanction modernization. As these new views threatened established interests, the mavericks attracted anger and repression. In China's case, Qing authorities condemned Kang's writings and made efforts to prevent their spread.

Kang became still more strident following the Sino-Japanese War. He led hundreds of civil service examination candidates in protest against the Treaty of Shimonoseki, founding study societies and publishing newspapers—themselves daring innovations—to promote his call for thoroughgoing institutional reform. Owing partly to Kang, reform was in the air in China in the late 1890s as never before.

The Hundred Days of Reform

Kang Youwei's calls for change bore fruit in an unexpected way. During the early 1890s, China's **Emperor Guangxu** was steadily emerging from the regency of his aunt, the Empress Dowager Cixi. Following defeat in the Sino-Japanese War, Guangxu's tutor exposed him to reformist ideas and directed his attention to Kang's writings. As the scramble for concessions proceeded, a crisis atmosphere gripped the capital and Guangxu became eager to take action. In June 1898, Kang used a personal audience with Guangxu to encourage him to take the initiative by creating new, modern-style laws and institutions in the manner of Japan.

Under the influence of Kang and other Confucian reformists, Guangxu proceeded to do exactly this. Over the next 103 days, Guangxu issued reform decrees covering such topics as the creation of modern schools, the revision of the civil service exams, the development of modern agriculture, and the construction of railroads—virtually an itemization of the changes Sun Yatsen had sought in his 1894 letter to Li Hongzhang. What made the program increasingly controversial was that it aimed squarely at the privileges of powerful groups within the Qing state. Their interests threatened, conservatives turned to Cixi, who maneuvered to bring the **Hundred Days of Reform**, as they became known, to an end. Cixi had Guangxu confined on an isolated island for the rest of his life—even as he remained officially "emperor." She also resumed control of the government and restored the *status quo ante*. The Hundred Days of Reform had ended in failure.

The end of reform spelled danger for the reformers, six of whom were quickly beheaded by the Qing government. Meanwhile, Kang and his foremost disciple, **Liang Qichao**, quietly escaped to nearby Japan. Thus, by the end of 1898, China's preeminent revolutionary, Sun Yatsen, and its main Confucian reformists—Kang and Liang—were all in Japan, a country that would play a critical role in the gestation of China's revolution.

4

Sun in Meiji Japan

During Sun Yatsen's first years in Japan, events in China moved rapidly. As the nineteenth century neared its end, the Chinese living in coastal spheres of influence were swiftly exposed to jarring new conditions. One especially heavily affected area was the northeastern province of Shandong, Confucius' revered birthplace. Coming under Germany's partial control, the province quickly experienced such ill-effects as Christian missionary attacks on Chinese civil and religious traditions and a German-built railroad that eliminated tens of thousands of local jobs. The added injury of flooding followed by drought helped provoke the rise of one of the most famous movements of modern Chinese history: the Boxers.

The Boxer movement received its name from mystical exercises that its members performed, some of which were purported to give them an immunity to bullets. Initially anti-Manchu, the Qing government was able to redirect the movement's prejudices against Westerners, and more especially, against privileged Chinese Christians, whom it singled out for repeated attacks. While local authorities suppressed the Boxers in Shandong, they soon reappeared in an aggravated form in Beijing. There they laid siege to the "Peking Legation"—the district of Beijing where prominent foreigners resided. Remarkably, the Qing government approved the siege and declared war on the foreign nations whose residents lived in the Legation! In response, seven of those nations—Japan, Russia, Great Britain, the United States, France, Austria, and Italy—created a sizable army to rescue the hostages. When this expeditionary force reached Beijing, it lifted the siege and occupied the imperial palace while committing numerous outrages against the Chinese population. The official end of the uprising came with the Boxer Protocol of 1901, which imposed a crushing indemnity on the Qing government and permanently stationed foreign troops on Chinese soil between Beijing and the sea.

During the **Boxer Uprising**, the Qing court took refuge in central China. Returning to Beijing in late 1901, it recognized clearly that China would have to modernize rapidly if the government was to have any chance of staying in power. To this end, the Empress Dowager Cixi announced a series of **New Policies** aimed at eradicating opium, creating public schools, modernizing the military, promulgating a constitution, and so on. Indeed, the policies included virtually everything that Cixi had rejected just three years earlier when she suppressed the Hundred Days of Reform in 1898. Ironically, while the Boxers had attempted to restore Chinese tradition, their failure to expel the foreigners had underscored just how badly China needed to modernize if it was to escape being "sliced up like a melon."

The Japanese Model

As the oft-repeated melon metaphor indicates, many educated Chinese at the turn of the twentieth century had begun to fear the possibility of national extinction. Their newspapers repeatedly compared China's plight with those of Turkey, Poland, India, Hawaii, and American Indian nations. It is in this context that many Chinese, including Sun Yatsen, turned to the neighboring country of Japan as a model of how to succeed in the modern world.

Actually, Sun had appreciated the Japanese example early, referring to Japan's accomplishments and utilizing its government's motto—"rich country, strong army"—in his 1894 letter to Li Hongzhang. Among reformists, the real surge in interest in Japan came after the Sino-Japanese War of 1894–1895; indeed, their Hundred Days of Reform comprised an attempt to repeat Japan's success within China. The core of the Qing government, on the other hand, had little interest in Japan until after the failure of the Boxer Uprising in 1900. At that point, the Japanese example became attractive because that country had managed to modernize while retaining its monarchical system—exactly what the Qing government now wanted to do. As a result, such New Policies as the new school system, the new army, and the new constitution would all bear the imprint of the Japanese model.

It is ironic that many Chinese were beginning to look enviously upon Japan. More than a thousand years earlier, after all, elite Japanese had turned to *China* as their primary model of civilization, absorbing such elements of Chinese culture as Confucian political institutions, Buddhist beliefs, and the complex character system that Japanese continue to use with modifications to write the Japanese language. In any event, this early massive cultural borrowing had not effaced salient characteristics of Japanese life, as the Japanese emperor—contrasting with the Chinese emperor—became a ritual figurehead and medieval Japan became a land ruled by the samurai military class.

During the early nineteenth century, when the Western impact began to be felt in East Asia, Japan was governed by a complexly organized feudal system. This system left it ill-prepared to defend itself against the Western powers, which in the 1850s imposed "unequal treaties" on Japan similar to those that they had recently imposed on Qing China. These treaties sparked fierce struggles within Japan, as xenophobic samurai began a campaign of assassinations aimed at government officials and Western businesspeople. These samurai claimed that the Japanese government's compromises with Westerners ran counter to the will of the emperor, Japan's ultimate ruler. Significantly, they called themselves "men of determination"—the same term Sun Yatsen later used in the Hong Kong oath of the Revive China Society.

Convinced through Western reprisals that simple resistance was impractical, the "men of determination" shifted course and employed Western military technology to overthrow their government. This *coup d'état*, known to history as the **Meiji Restoration**, occurred in 1868. Following the Restoration, leaders of samurai background undertook the rapid modernization of Japan in the name of a young new emperor—the Emperor Meiji—whose reign lasted until his death in 1912.

The ensuing Meiji transformation was the most successful effort at modernization on the part of a non-Western people during the nineteenth century. The keynote of this effort was government centralization, as Meiji leaders rapidly replaced feudal arrangements with a modern bureaucracy, a unified conscript army, and a nationwide land tax. Alongside these changes, the government spurred the growth of strategic industries and spread scientific knowledge through public schools and trade associations.

The Meiji government had understood, as China's Self-Strengtheners had not, that successful modernization required a sustained commitment to industrial and educational infrastructure. The government also understood that a degree of political change was inevitable, and to that end it promulgated a modern constitution—the first in Asia—that established a parliament and elections with limited suffrage. At its best, then, the sociopolitical system that had taken shape in Meiji Japan by the 1890s smoothly combined stability with flexibility. This combination directly contributed to Japan's victory in the Sino-Japanese War, in recognition of which the Western powers gradually abrogated their "unequal treaties" with Japan and began to treat it as a near-equal.

Sun Meets Miyazaki

Sun Yatsen would spend almost 10 years of his adult life in Japan, rendering it truly his second home, after China, in the length of time he resided there. While his travel schedule was sometimes frenetic, he spent long stretches of time in Japan, particularly during the period from 1897 to 1905. That he was able to use that country as his base of operations owed much to his friendships with certain well-placed Japanese who took a deep interest in mainland Asian affairs.

During the early decades of the Meiji period, the Japanese elite had sought to separate Japan from the mainland of Asia and to identify it instead with the successful modern West. Nevertheless, the sheer geographical proximity of Japan to mainland Asia guaranteed that Japanese would remain vitally interested in regional conditions. They were especially concerned about Western expansion—for example, Russian expansion into northeast Asia—as such expansion might prefigure an attempt to colonize Japan. In addition, as their modernization progressed, Japanese increasingly viewed themselves as having escaped from the "backward" circumstances in which their neighbors were still mired. Historian Marius Jansen has summarized the resulting outlook: "Since Japan had freed herself, she was the logical candidate to help her neighbors. This was a theme that lent itself equally well to idealism, opportunism, and chauvinism." Indeed, idealism could shade into opportunism and chauvinism almost imperceptibly, as Japan's strength and Asia's well-being became subtly intermingled in the minds of many Japanese.

A number of figures at various points along Meiji Japan's political spectrum actively promoted the cause of reform in mainland Asia. Prominent examples include the parliamentary politician Inukai Tsuyoshi, the rightist powerbroker Tôyama Mitsuru, and the continental adventurer **Miyazaki Tôten**—all of whom became friends with Sun Yatsen. Regardless of the differences among them, all of these figures opposed Western expansion on the Asian mainland and viewed indigenous modernization movements in Asian nations as an essential preventive to such expansion. This pan-Asianist outlook predisposed them to welcome Sun's call for political and technological revolution in China and to lobby actively on his behalf with Japanese officials.

Sun's closest and longest friendship with any Japanese citizen was the one he enjoyed with Miyazaki Tôten. Miyazaki was born into a large ex-samurai family in Japan's restive south. As a child, he was exposed to both liberal ideals and a steady stream of stories of past heroes. Perhaps as a result, he converted to Christianity, passionate in this as in everything he did. His brother Yazô convinced him that he should devote himself to saving Asia from Western imperialism, and from that point onward, his major challenge was to find a way to express this ambition in meaningful action. His first several attempts, involving contacts in Korea and Thailand, respectively, ended in failure. Then in 1897, he met Sun Yatsen.

Despite their difference in nationality, Sun and Miyazaki shared a similar background: Each had a Western education, experience with Christianity, close brushes with poverty, and a willingness to act outside of the law. In short, they were marginal figures within their respective societies. Fittingly, they first met in one of Japan's treaty ports, Yokohama, where Sun was organizing among local Chinese following his tumultuous stay in London.

Miyazaki brought great expectations to his encounter with Sun: He had already heard about him from his friends and had wondered whether he might be the "man of determination" who could revitalize China. The way he met Sun was through Chen Shaobai, then residing in Yokohama. Miyazaki had visited Chen's house one evening and had learned that a guest was staying at the house. When Miyazaki returned the next morning, he met the guest—Sun—and struggled to control his disappointment. Miyazaki later described the scene: "He had not rinsed his mouth or washed his face, and he sat there just the way he'd gotten out of bed. At first I was startled by such casualness, and thought he must be rather unstable." Judging by external appearance alone, Miyazaki had trouble imagining that this man could really "take power over four hundred million Chinese . . ."

After Sun washed and changed his clothes, they resumed their meeting, though Miyazaki still felt that Sun somehow lacked dignity. The two men had difficulty communicating, as Miyazaki knew little English or Chinese and Sun knew little Japanese. Nevertheless, they conversed through the words they both knew, supplementing their speech with the characters that are used to write Chinese and Japanese alike. As they exchanged views they warmed to each other. In Miyazaki's description, Sun "became more and more impassioned and enthusiastic, and by the time he finished the gentleman who had begun so carefully was more like a tiger growling deep in the mountains." Sun's basic message was that for China to become strong, it needed a republican system of government, which it had had in the distant past and

Sun Yatsen, far right, posed with several Japanese friends
in 1899. Miyazaki Tôten stands at the center of the photo.
(*Courtesy of the Library of Congress*)

which it could have again in the future if a hero arose to overthrow the Manchus.
Miyazaki listened raptly throughout: "How noble his thought, how sharp his
insight, how great his conception, how burning his fervor! . . . he is a precious jewel
of Asia." Miyazaki henceforth became a lifelong follower and placed his numerous
contacts in the Japanese government at Sun's disposal.

Indeed, doors began to open for Sun after he met and impressed Miyazaki: He
was soon introduced to Tōyama and Inukai, developing an especially close relationship with the latter. With the help of Miyazaki and his friends, Sun developed
a cover identity as a language teacher and moved to a house in Tokyo, Japan's
capital. His cover was necessary to satisfy the Japanese government, which hesitated to shelter an avowed enemy of the Chinese government, as well as to ward
off the Chinese government, which continued to spy on Sun and might seek to
assassinate him. As part of his cover, Sun adopted "Nakayama" as his Japanese
name. Pronounced in Chinese, the characters of this name read as "Zhongshan."
Meaning "central mountain," this is the primary name by which Sun is known
throughout the Chinese-speaking world.

We saw in Chapter 3 that when China's Hundred Days of Reform ended in failure
in the fall of 1898, reformists who could escape made their way to Japan. There they
received a hero's welcome. Indeed, Kang Youwei, their leader, was treated as though
he led a government-in-exile: He stayed at the house of Japan's prime minister and
was entertained by an imperial prince and other notables. Kang hoped that the
Japanese government would help him overthrow the Empress Dowager Cixi straight-
away, so Emperor Guangxu could resume his implementation of a reformist program
for China. While clearly favoring Kang's cause, however, the Japanese government
did not wish to intervene in China's internal affairs in such a peremptory manner.

Overall, Japanese officials were distinctly more comfortable with the reformists,
who sought to maintain China's monarchical system with adjustments, than with

the revolutionaries, who aimed to replace that system entirely with a republic. This is not surprising, given that Japan itself was a monarchy and that worldwide, monarchies still far outnumbered republics at the end of the nineteenth century. Despite their leanings, however, Japanese officials did seek change in China, and they felt that the best way to facilitate it was to bring the reformists and the revolutionaries together to form a united front. To that end, Inukai invited Sun and Kang to meet together at his house for discussions. Sun attended but Kang sent his disciple Liang Qichao instead. Sun and Liang got along well and agreed to seek grounds for cooperation between their respective groups. At a follow-up meeting at Kang's lodgings 2 days later, however, Kang insisted that he had come to Japan on behalf of the emperor and sought only to return him to power. Subsequently, Kang never showed any inclination to cooperate with the revolutionaries.

Liang Qichao, on the other hand, remained interested. After Kang left Japan in spring 1899 to seek aid in Canada, Liang stayed behind and resumed his acquaintance with Sun. Nevertheless, when Kang ordered Liang at the end of 1899 to leave Japan for Hawaii to support his reformist organization there, Liang obeyed him. In mid-1900, one last effort was made to bring the reformists and the revolutionaries together. On that occasion, Miyazaki, representing Sun, visited Kang, who now lived in the British colony of Singapore. Kang thought that Miyazaki's visit was a trap and that Sun was trying to have him assassinated! Accordingly, he contacted the Singapore police, who arrested Miyazaki and escorted him out of the colony. Sun's patience with the reformists was finally exhausted. What he had once said of Kang in frustration he now held as his general view: "That rotten Confucianist is worthless."

The Huizhou Uprising

While Sun continued to base his operations in Japan, the Boxer Uprising took place in 1900. As someone who continually sought to exploit the Qing government's misfortunes, he eagerly followed news of the uprising and the ensuing disorder. Indeed, his greatest difficulty lay in figuring out how to play his revolutionary cards: Should he ally with southern Chinese governors who were defying Qing orders to support the Boxers, or should he ally with foreign governments that were scheming for new gains at the Qing government's expense? While he made offers of future rewards to virtually all parties—even Li Hongzhang—to attract their support, he would rely in the end on assistance from Japan.

Sun had been planning for some time to launch a revolt with the help of secret societies in central China. In early 1900, however, the main secret society of the region shifted its allegiance to the reformists, who had offered it more money. As a result, Sun had to turn his attention back to the south, where his friend Zheng Shiliang maintained close contacts with the Triads. Sun, Miyazaki, and other conspirators selected the city of Huizhou, roughly 100 miles east of Guangzhou, as their initial target, with the intent of proceeding to Guangzhou in force once they had captured it. Traveling among overseas Chinese communities in Southeast Asia, Sun had his usual difficulties acquiring money and weapons for

Singapore etc.

the operation. Zheng, meanwhile, had managed to recruit a number of local Triads for the cause. When attacked in the mountains by government troops in October, Zheng's rebel force won, beginning a string of victories for them. As the rebels approached Huizhou, however, Sun sent them a surprising message: Instead of capturing Huizhou and heading west, they should travel 250 miles *east* to Xiamen. Xiamen was a large city on the southeast coast facing the island of Taiwan, then a Japanese colony. The Japanese governor-general of Taiwan had promised Sun assistance—money and weapons—should his forces appear in Xiamen, so Sun wanted them to travel there.

For its part, Zheng's rebel army was growing as it passed through friendly villages, reaching as many as 20,000 men at its maximum. Even so, the terrain was becoming less familiar. In addition, Sun was having difficulties with the Japanese, who were retreating from their earlier plans to capture the Xiamen region. Lacking their help, Sun reluctantly terminated the campaign while Zheng's army was still over a hundred miles away from Xiamen. Afterward, most of the rebels quickly faded back into the countryside. However, Yamada Yoshimasa, a Japanese courier for Sun, was captured and executed by government troops, making him, in Sun's words, "the first foreigner who sacrificed his life on the altar of the Chinese revolution."

Despite the desultory end to the **Huizhou Uprising**, it marked the first time that an army actually fought in China on behalf of Sun's revolutionary cause. It also showed how attractive that cause could be, as rebels passed through villages receiving warm welcomes and swelling their numbers. If the countryside, where the overwhelming majority of the Chinese lived, was this receptive to the idea of revolution, perhaps the overthrow of the Qing dynasty was not such a long ways off.

Sun's Japan Connection

Sun's link with Japan would remain strong throughout the remainder of his life. Despite this, Japanese (aside from Miyazaki) did not always give him good reason for his continued loyalty. The Japanese government never provided his forces—or in 1912, his government—with weapons. It also rarely supported his political objectives publicly. As Marius Jansen suggests, Japanese officials usually turned to Sun only when other options, such as relations with the government or moderate reformers, were closed for some reason. Moreover, during the 1910s and beyond, the Japanese government would become sharply focused on seeking Japan's advantages in China with little concern for the Chinese people or even the opinions of its Western allies. In hindsight, this behavior presages Japan's later horrific invasion of China during World War II, which has rendered the very subject of Sun's friendship with Japan highly awkward among Chinese.

Yet while many of Sun's Chinese revolutionary friends became strongly anti-Japanese in the 1910s and later, Sun remained convinced that Japan was, or should be, China's friend. A famous speech that he gave in Kobe, Japan, in late 1924, less than 4 months before his death, ends with the following words:

> Japan today has become acquainted with the Western civilization of the rule of Might, but retains the characteristics of the Oriental civilization of the rule of Right. Now the question remains whether Japan will be the hawk of the Western civilization of the rule of Might, or the tower of strength of the Orient. This is the choice which lies before the people of Japan.

Sun biographer Harold Schiffrin points out that in Sun's appeal to the Japanese "there was a unique warmth and fervor, and above all, a frankness which is missing in comparable claims on the British." For the British, he had to play the gentleman and the proponent of free trade, while among the Japanese—especially marginal Japanese like Miyazaki—he could be himself. Indeed, when he would speak at Japanese banquets in the 1910s, he would typically begin by stating, "If there were Europeans here tonight, they would not be able to tell the Chinese from the Japanese. Japan is my second home, and I regard this as a family reunion." While he sometimes criticized Japanese imperialism in China, he remained convinced that Japan essentially served as "the watchman of Asia," protecting it against Western aggression.

Sun even identified his own movement to overthrow Manchu rule with the samurai movement that overthrew Japan's feudal system. As he once declared to a Japanese audience regarding his Chinese comrades, "We are the 'men of determination' of the Meiji Restoration of fifty years ago."

CHAPTER

5

Creating the Revolutionary Alliance

Students often play important roles in movements for change worldwide. Most adults are wedded to the world as it is: They have bills to pay, aging parents and children to care for, and profitable relationships to maintain. In contrast, many college students are young and unmarried, so the thick web of stabilizing relationships has not yet woven its way around them. They are freer to be voices of conscience, voices of extremism—or an unsteady mixture of both. In China, a school-centered student culture began to take shape during the first decade of the twentieth century. Previously, those Chinese wealthy enough to afford a formal education received most of that education from tutors. At the beginning of the twentieth century, however, the Chinese government would foster a school-centered culture for the nation's best and brightest. This culture, intended to promote professional talent, unwittingly nurtured a contempt for much that was old and an eagerness for all that was new—especially new and Western. This would give Sun Yatsen, ever on the lookout for dissatisfied Chinese, essential new opportunities to advance his revolutionary agenda.

Chinese Students in Tokyo

With the failure of the Boxer Uprising, it was clear to all politically significant forces in China that large-scale changes were inevitable. There was still the pressing question, however, as to how far the changes would go. The Qing government hoped to contain the need for change somewhat with its New Policies—which were nevertheless radical departures in their own right. The reformists sought to take the changes all the way to the brink of revolution while retaining the emperor as at least the symbolic ruler over China. Revolutionaries like Sun Yatsen, in turn, wanted to press revolution to its logical conclusion, namely, the replacement of an emperor-centered political system with a republic. Young elite Chinese, anxious about China's future and freed from the traditional educational system, had to decide which path they would support.

Let us examine the changes in education more carefully since they form the backdrop for Sun's effort to attract students to his cause. As Confucianism has always stressed education, it was fitting that several of the Qing government's most important New Policies addressed the subject directly. The government moved quickly to change the context of instruction in China by building new schools, teaching new subjects, and modifying the civil service examinations that aspirants for public office took. In 1905, the government made a fateful further step: It abolished the traditional examination system altogether. This sparked a massive new trend, as thousands of youths from wealthy families across China headed abroad for the higher educations that would advance their future careers. Owing to its proximity, affordability, and similar written language, the country that the majority of these youths selected for their studies was Japan.

Marius Jansen points out that from a global perspective, Chinese student migration to Meiji Japan was the first large-scale movement of students from one nation to another in modern times. The statistics tell the story: From a mere 13 Chinese students in Japan in 1896, the number swelled to 500 in 1902 and 8,000 in 1905, following which it slowly declined. Eight thousand students (a conservative estimate, by the way) was an impressive concentration in a single foreign country—especially when contrasted with the mere dozens of Chinese who were studying in Europe and the United States.

The Chinese student community in Japan possessed several striking characteristics. First, many of the Chinese students were funded by provincial government scholarships, owing to the ominous fact that the provinces were far more solvent than the debt-ridden Qing government was. Second, the students tended to focus on the humanities or military studies, as less politically minded science and engineering students typically opted for Europe or the United States. Third, some of the students were females—an unprecedented circumstance in Chinese history and a sign of how much had already changed. Finally, a number of students failed to enroll in a college at all! What they did instead was participate in the active Chinese student community, which was concentrated in the bustling Kanda district of Tokyo. This convergence of students in a single location contrasts sharply with the experiences of past Chinese generations, whose ambitious youth ordinarily studied in isolation within their families' walled compounds. Not surprisingly, the in-gathering at Kanda had the effect of providing Sun Yatsen with an ideal environment for recruitment.

The New Climate of Opinion

Initially, the figure who most attracted Chinese students in Tokyo as the student population surged was Liang Qichao, the wayward disciple of Kang Youwei. Liang, we recall, had participated in the Hundred Days of Reform in 1898, after which he escaped to Japan. Remaining in that country for nearly all of the next 14 years, he would become the most influential Chinese writer of his generation through passionate essays he composed on virtually all aspects of China's twentieth-century predicament.

The apogee of Liang's influence came in 1902 and 1903. At this time, his primary theme was that China needed "new citizens" in order to thrive in the modern world. According to him, past Chinese generations had been fatalistic and focused on individual gain. These traits spelled failure in modern times, when successful governments were mobilizing the energies of entire peoples in their ceaseless struggles against one another. China, as one country among others, needed to learn to compete, and this would require changes not simply at the levels of technology or institutions, but above all at the level of the mind-set—the morality—of the Chinese people. Henceforth, the Chinese would have to identify with China, that is, with each other. As he dramatically stated,

> We must have ten thousand eyes with one sight, ten thousand hands and feet with only one mind, ten thousand ears with one hearing, ten thousand powers with only one purpose in life; then the state is established ten-thousand-fold strong. When mind touches mind, when power is linked to power, cog to cog, strand around strand, and ten thousand roads meet in one center, this will be a nation-state.

Liang was influenced by social Darwinism in his vision of modern imperialism as an endless competition between tough, activist peoples. At the same time, he also displayed a lingering Confucianism in his insistence that *morality*—in this case, the morality of complete identification with one's group—is the core issue for every society upon which its final success depends.

There are many points of overlap between Liang and Sun: For example, both men foresaw the need for a sustained mobilization of the Chinese people to meet the Western challenge. Yet there were important differences as well. The single greatest difference is that Liang was a gradualist: He strongly believed in evolutionary progress, with the consequence that he opposed the idea that China could skip what he viewed as necessary historical stages. Sun, in contrast, was impatient to see China advance to the forefront of the world's nations, politically as well as technologically. He expressed this view through a locomotive analogy that he employed in numerous speeches. When borrowing technology from abroad, he argued, it is not necessary to repeat all the stages of development of that technology. For example, it is not necessary for China to construct early style locomotives before it can acquire the latest model. Rather, it can employ the latest model without any delay. Likewise, he argued, China need not experience constitutional monarchy for a set period of years before moving on to a republican form of government. Rather, it should adopt the latest foreign model of government—republicanism—right away. So far as the rapidity of change is concerned, Chinese students abroad in the first decade of the twentieth century would increasingly support Sun's call for revolution against Liang's trust in evolution.

One author who put a sharp twist on Liang's emphasis on activity over passivity was the precocious Zou Rong. At age 18, Zou wrote *The Revolutionary Army*, a tract that helped spread the message of revolution through the student community in Tokyo and far beyond. Zou's main argument was that Chinese passivity was a product of oppressive Manchu rule. If Chinese people band together and immediately eliminate Manchu rule, they will become masters of their own destiny, ready to stand up to Western imperialism—the *second* foreign menace. The opening sentence of *The Revolutionary Army* provides a fine example of its intemperate rhetoric:

> Sweep away millennia of despotism in all its forms, throw off millennia of slavishness, annihilate the five million and more of the furry and horned Manchu race, cleanse ourselves of 260 years of harsh and unremitting pain, so that the soil of the Chinese subcontinent is made immaculate, and the descendants of the Yellow Emperor will all become Washingtons.

To underscore the need to oust the Manchus, Zou dwelt on the brutality with which the Manchus had conquered China in the seventeenth century. He also appealed to a traditional pride in Chinese civilization (mixed with some pseudo-scientific racism): "Is not the unchanging norm of race that which distinguishes the kinsmen and fellowcountrymen of our great Han race from barbarians of the North, South, East and West?" While he displayed a racist contempt for the Manchus, however, he felt more ambivalent regarding the West, as his positive reference to George Washington indicates. Indeed, despite his hostility toward Western imperialism, he argued toward the end of *The Revolutionary Army* that China should model its government after that of the United States.

Sun Yatsen quickly decided that *The Revolutionary Army* would serve as a useful recruiting tool for him. While distancing himself from Zou's call for the physical annihilation of the Manchu people, Sun nevertheless had thousands of copies of the tract printed for free distribution to overseas Chinese living in San Francisco and Singapore. Large numbers of Chinese elsewhere eagerly read the work as well, to the point that by 1911, it had run through some 20 editions and sold a million copies! Other authors soon repeated Zou's anti-Manchu nationalistic sentiments, giving them still greater exposure.

Despite the rising popularity of anti-Manchu Chinese nationalism during the first decade of the twentieth century, there were several ironies that such a nationalism—Sun's own nationalism at this time—could never escape. First, the reasoning was evasive. While insisting that the Manchus had either harmed China themselves or had helped Westerners harm China, the line of argument carefully avoided acknowledging any Chinese responsibility for China's situation. That is, by exaggerating the cruelty of some Manchus, anti-Manchu nationalists were trying to escape the uncomfortable fact that their own forebears had failed to protect their country against Western depredations. Second, the reasoning was often insincere. Thus, while Zou doubtlessly meant what he wrote, most anti-Manchu nationalists knew very well that the Manchus were not really the main cause of China's difficulties. By playing a crude race card, they hoped to provoke a political change—the overthrow of the Qing dynasty—that they did not seem able to bring about any other way. Finally, the reasoning created a shallow and misleading unity. While various Chinese might agree on eliminating Manchu rule, they did not agree on what sort of government China should have after they succeeded. Anti-Manchu nationalism allowed these Chinese to work together in the short term while putting off for later all of the hard effort of creating a viable future for their country.

The Russo-Japanese War

While Chinese students in Tokyo were refining their nationalistic arguments, East Asia underwent another convulsion that reminded the Chinese people yet again of their vulnerability to outside forces. The convulsion was the **Russo-Japanese War** (1904–1905), which Russia and Japan fought over future control of the Korean peninsula.

Ten years earlier, Meiji Japan had waged the Sino-Japanese War to prevent China from achieving control over Korea. This time around, the Japanese government was convinced that Russia, rather than China, was poised to take over that country. As it wanted to keep Korea out of foreign hands (besides its own) at all costs, it concluded a military alliance with Great Britain in 1902 and launched a surprise attack on a nearby Russian naval base in early 1904. Although both sides—Japan and Russia—suffered major losses in the war that ensued, Japan emerged victorious after a lopsided victory against Russia's ailing Baltic Fleet. The treaty signed at the war's conclusion in 1905 gave Japan control over Korea's foreign affairs, a stipulation that rapidly led to Japan's colonization of that country.

The broadest significance of the Russo-Japanese War is that it demonstrated for the first time that a non-Western nation could defeat a Western one using modern weapons. Sun personally witnessed the importance of this. In his 1924 speech in Kobe, Japan, he recounted an ocean voyage he took from Europe to Southeast Asia shortly after the war ended:

> When the steamer passed the Suez Canal [in British-controlled Egypt] a number of natives came to see me. All of them wore smiling faces, and asked me whether I was a Japanese. I replied that I was a Chinese, and inquired what was on their minds, and why they were so happy. They said they had just heard the news that Japan had completely destroyed the Russian fleet recently despatched from Europe . . .

Sun's reportage suggests the larger mood throughout much of Asia, where Japan's victory boosted morale and galvanized anti-colonialist movements. At the same time, the victory also impressed the Qing government, prompting it to accelerate the implementation of its New Policies. And it especially struck the Chinese students in Tokyo, who were astonished at the intense patriotism displayed by ordinary Japanese. Liang Qichao's call for a nationalistically unified China—for "ten thousand powers with only one purpose in life"—seemed ever more compelling in light of what Meiji Japan's nationalism was able to achieve.

The Birth of the Revolutionary Alliance

Between the Boxer Uprising in 1900 and the abolition of the civil service examination system in 1905, many Chinese students in Japan had read and adopted views similar to those of Sun Yatsen, namely, that China needed political revolution as well as technological modernization. Despite this, the relationship between the Sun and the students developed slowly. The biggest obstacle was social: Sun came from a peasant background, while the students came from some of the most distinguished families in all of China. Reformists had told the students that Sun could not even read Chinese characters! This was untrue, as the students learned.

Nevertheless, at least initially the students found Sun's close relations with secret societies and overseas Chinese merchants disquieting. The students regarded themselves as members of an elite with a long-standing relationship to political power. In contrast, secret societies and overseas merchants struck them as quite marginal: How could people from such backgrounds rescue China from its predicament? Sun, in turn, had his own problems with the students. His main interest lay in accumulating funds and troops for future uprisings. What access could mere students have to such things?

As the two sides began to learn more about each other, they gradually shed some of their earlier concerns. The students learned that Sun possessed an extensive Western education, a long history of revolutionary activity, and a gentlemanly demeanor—all characteristics that they lacked and could employ for their cause. They were very worried that a prolonged revolution might provide Western nations with an excuse to divide China among themselves. With a talented leader like Sun, they reasoned, the revolution would probably take place quickly and the Western nations, in turn, would respond with restraint. Sun, for his part, came to recognize that at least some students had become serious about organizing uprisings and that they could provide him with access to more regions of China.

As the Russo-Japanese War was reaching its conclusion in spring 1905, Sun traveled to Europe and attracted Chinese students there to his revolutionary proposals. Upon returning to Japan, his friend Miyazaki introduced him to **Huang Xing** and **Song Jiaoren**, two figures who would play major roles in Sun's future. Huang was the founder of the China Arise Society, an underground revolutionary group that fomented rebellions in the central Yangzi valley region of China. Song, in turn, was a leading member of this group, which consisted primarily of present and former Chinese students in Japan. Sun and Huang quickly agreed to join forces and create a broad new organization for those Chinese seeking to overthrow the Qing dynasty.

The result was the founding of the **Revolutionary Alliance** in August 1905 with Sun Yatsen as its president and Huang Xing as its vice president. A huge celebration, attended by more than a thousand Chinese students, was held to honor Sun at a Tokyo restaurant on August 13. Following Miyazaki's words of welcome, Sun captivated his audience with a fiery nationalistic speech that promised the rapid restoration of Chinese greatness. A week later, the Revolutionary Alliance was formally inaugurated and several hundred students were eagerly sworn in.

The creation of the Revolutionary Alliance was a momentous event in the history of the Chinese revolution. The Alliance was created out of four prior organizations, including the Revive China Society, Sun's earlier organization. It was substantially different from the Revive China Society, however. The Revive China Society had only been active prior to revolts, namely, the Guangzhou revolt of 1895 and the Huizhou revolt of 1900. The Society had few branches and it appealed primarily to Christian, Western-educated southern Chinese. In contrast, the Revolutionary Alliance was continually active (if sometimes chaotic) and created a wide network of branches in China, Japan, Southeast Asia, and North America. Its members came from various parts of China and various social classes: While students of scholar-gentry background dominated initially, they were joined over time by numerous overseas Chinese businessmen. The Revolutionary Alliance also had a more sophisticated philosophy than the Revive China Society did. Whereas the Revive China Society had simply called for the overthrow of the Manchus and the replacement of their dynasty with a republic, the Revolutionary Alliance obliged its members to swear allegiance to something called the **Three People's Principles**. Sun formulated these principles himself, insisting that they were essential to the future creation of a stronger and more equitable China. The principles were nationalism, democracy, and **people's livelihood**. Sun promoted these three principles for the remaining two decades of his life, and they are the catchphrases that tens of millions of Chinese recall as soon as they hear the name "Sun Zhongshan." It is to them that we now turn.

Planning China's Future

When Chinese people think of Sun Yatsen, they think not only of his political activities but also of his ideas regarding China's ideal future path. He expressed these ideas across two decades, from shortly prior to the formation of the Revolutionary Alliance in 1905 all the way until his death in 1925. Invariably, Sun's speeches and writings during these decades would return to a single theme, namely, the importance of what he called the Three People's Principles for the development of a united, progressive China. Especially after his death, successive governments in China promoted these principles, with the result that their basic meaning is familiar to virtually all Chinese today. Accordingly, this chapter interrupts our chronological journey through Sun's life to take a more detailed look at the principles and what Sun conveyed by them.

The Three People's Principles in which Sun Yatsen took such pride are nationalism, democracy, and people's livelihood. In Chinese, these principles are expressed in three words, each of which contains two characters: *min-zu, min-quan,* and *min-sheng.* The character "min," which begins each principle, simply means "people," as in "citizens." So the principles literally translate as "people-tribe," "people-rights," and "people-life." Sun Yatsen once explained them by equating them with American President Abraham Lincoln's famous reference to "government of the people, by the people, for the people." He also viewed them as similar to the French Revolution's motto, "liberty, equality, fraternity" (though the order of Sun's principles places fraternity—i.e., nationalism—first). At least at one level, then, Sun wished to argue that his People's Principles were comparable to ideas that had already been circulating in the Western world.

Whether or not the principles themselves were original, Sun gave them special meanings that corresponded to his understanding of China's predicament in the early twentieth century. After first presenting the principles in late 1905, he continued to refine his explanations of them throughout the rest of his life. His most in-depth exposition appears in *The Three People's Principles,* a collection of 16 speeches he gave in 1924. This series of speeches juxtapose passages of careful explication with flights of fiery political rhetoric. Actually, the passion conveys a good deal about Sun's objective, which was not merely to convince his audience of his ideas but to excite it to the point that it would do whatever was necessary to preserve and strengthen China. As he asks in the very first lecture, "What is a principle? It is an idea, a faith, and a power." Despite vast changes in his circumstances, Sun's overall "faith" did not change greatly during the last two decades of his life. Consequently, the explanation of the Three People's Principles that appears in the rest of this chapter will take the 1924 speeches as his primary statement of their meaning.

The Principle of Nationalism

For Sun, everything begins with nationalism. China, he maintained, was in grave danger for its very existence. And as he saw matters, the only possible antidote was the spread of an unshakable nationalistic pride among the four hundred million people of the country. ("Four hundred million," a figure that appears repeatedly in Sun's writings, was China's estimated population during the early twentieth century. China's population a century later is more than triple this number.) By the 1920s, this apocalyptic view was somewhat less persuasive than it had been two decades earlier, inasmuch as the Western powers had shifted from expanding their privileges in China to simply maintaining them. Sun thus has to resort to special arguments to make his case. Highlighting economics—and especially the "**unequal treaties**"—he asserts that the position of China in the world in the 1920s is actually *lower* than that of a colony: ". . . we are being crushed by the economic strength of the Powers to a greater degree than if we were a full colony. China is not the colony of one nation but of all . . . I think we ought to be called a 'hypo-colony.'" He also argues, curiously, that China is in demographic danger. The danger, he maintains, is that the Western nations are rapidly increasing their populations while China's population remains stagnant. If this continues for another century, he asserts, "the more will subjugate the less and China will inevitably be swallowed up." While such a prediction has not proven correct, Sun's use of it clearly expresses his larger sense that the West continues to press in on China, threatening it with extinction at various levels.

Sun's solution to this is, of course, nationalism. China, he asserts, has both disadvantages and advantages in this regard. The major disadvantage is that many of the Chinese have traditionally lacked any sense of nationalism, concentrating their attention instead on the well-being of their families and clans. This disadvantage is offset by two important advantages. The first advantage, in his view, is that China's history marks the unique convergence of a state (the Chinese government) and a race (the Chinese people). In other countries, Sun holds, the state either rules over several different races or it rules over only part of a race—large portions of the race living under the jurisdiction of other governments. In China, contrastingly, state and race match fairly smoothly, so political loyalty and racial affinity (as he regarded it) reinforce each other.

China's second advantage in developing nationalism is that the very devotion of the Chinese to family and clan—particularly to clan—can help lay the groundwork for creating a strong modern state:

> . . . when two Chinese meet each other on the road, they will chat together and ask each other's "honorable surname" and "great name"; if they happen to

find that they are of the same clan, they become wonderfully intimate and cordial and look upon each other as uncle or brother of the same family. If this worthy clan sentiment could be expanded, we might develop nationalism out of clanism.

The reason that "clanism" is an advantage is that it provides structure between the levels of the individual and the state. As Sun states, "If we take the clans as our social units and, after improving their internal organization, join them together to form a state, our task will naturally be easier than that of foreign countries which make the individual the unit." In short, with clan as with "race," China's traditional development has provided especially effective bases on which Chinese leaders can forge a future national identity.

For Sun, it is beyond question that such an identity is necessary. The single most famous and frequently repeated image of China in *The Three People's Principles* is that of "a sheet of loose sand." According to Sun, individuals and groups within China have too much freedom—so much freedom that they no more notice it than they would notice the air they breathe—and this has inhibited their ability to accomplish anything on a unified basis. The solution is clear: Remove the freedom. As he phrases it, the Chinese "must break down individual liberty and become pressed together into an unyielding body like the firm rock which is formed by the addition of cement to sand." As unappealing as this may sound, it is the approach that most nationalists outside of the West have taken in the twentieth and twenty-first centuries: Unity in the face of foreign threats is typically more important to them than is the creation of societies that give individuals or groups the power to affect or resist the demands of the state.

Given his strong attachment to nationalism, Sun did not want to see Chinese people embrace "cosmopolitanism." Indeed, he explicitly cautioned against two sorts of cosmopolitanism: the older Chinese type that complacently regarded China as the ethical center of human civilization, and the newer Western type that persuades "wronged races" to put aside their legitimate grievances against the West. Despite his warnings regarding cosmopolitanism, however, Sun did not really abjure it for all time. Rather, he deferred it for a peaceable distant future, after nationalistic competition has run its course. In the view of Marie-Claire Bergère, this distant future has Chinese earmarks: "The world of justice that Sun evoked [for the long term] was to have China as its center and was to be founded on Confucian morality." Interestingly, his vision also displays the influence of then-popular Russian anarchist Peter Kropotkin, who held that mutual aid rather than survival of the fittest is the chief mechanism of biological evolution. Overall, Sun embraced nationalistic struggle as China's path for the tumultuous present. He did believe, however, that in the fullness of time a "great harmony" (*datong*) among peoples as based on mutual aid could be both hoped for and expected.

One special issue with regard to the principle of nationalism is Sun's view of minority peoples within China. The land area of China as established by the Qing dynasty contained several important minorities, including Manchus, Mongols, Tibetans, and Uighurs. These minorities together formed a small percentage of China's total population. Despite this, they comprised—and continue to comprise— the majority in geographically large areas, such as China's northeast, northwest, and southwest. What attitude should the Chinese majority take toward them? Should they be assimilated into China, given autonomy within China, or permitted to establish their own separate nations? The republican government that Sun briefly led in 1912, following the fall of the Qing dynasty, promoted a new national flag that was comprised of five colored bars, one representing each of the main peoples of China. As this suggests, Sun supported assimilation of the minorities into China with a residual recognition of their distinctiveness within the country. Such an approach has two sides. On the one hand, Sun appears fair-minded toward the minorities with his invitation to them to share in the benefits of citizenship in modern China. For example, he pointedly rejected the option of taking revenge against the Manchu people after their dynastic rule over China had ended. On the other hand, there is an implicit condescension in Sun's position: Even as he welcomed the minorities into China, he could not assign their indigenous cultures any special value in a China that, after all, "belonged" ultimately to the Chinese. This skittish approach—tolerant yet hegemonic—has left a lasting legacy, shaping and sometimes warping relations between the Chinese majority and ethnic minorities within China down to the present day.

The Principle of Democracy

For Sun, everything comes back to nationalism and the principle of democracy is no exception. Nationalistic pride urges him to find precedents for democracy in Chinese history, while nationalistic anxiety urges him to restrict the practice of democracy in certain ways so as to minimize its fractiousness and maximize its efficiency. Overall, what he most appreciates about democracy is that it encourages ordinary citizens to have a sense of participation in the affairs and future of their country. When citizens acquire that sense of participation, he believes, they will be more willing to make sacrifices in order to increase their country's strength.

Traditionally, China did not possess a democracy, inasmuch as dynastic governments did not hold elections for public office. Sun claims, however, that the concern for the well-being of the public that characterizes democracies also characterized ancient China. Invoking the legendary sage-kings Yao and Shun, Sun remarks that "[a]lthough their government was autocratic in name, yet in reality they gave the people power. . . ." In the same vein, he highlights Confucian humanism, contending that Confucius advocated "people's rights" more than 2,000 years ago. In short, he maintains that ancient China had some democratic values. If it adopts democratic institutions in modern times, it will be elaborating on an aspect of its own traditions rather than simply importing a successful model from beyond its borders.

While revitalizing its ancient traditions, Sun argues, China should avoid repeating the West's recent mistakes. Western democracies, he holds, have fostered an unfortunate attitude of "opposition to government" among the peoples over whom they rule. Sun wishes to discourage the growth of such an attitude in China by distinguishing—as he believes Western governments have not done—between "sovereignty" and "ability." Clearly, the people need to be sovereign. In language reminiscent of Liang Qichao, he stated, "When we have a real republic, who will be king? The people, our four hundred millions, will be king." However, the people do not have the ability to actually administer the nation. Indeed, "the great majority [of Chinese] are those who have no vision or foresight." What they should do is entrust the day-to-day administration of government to a band of individuals who *do* have vision and foresight. At one point, Sun compares this to the relation between the general manager of a company and the shareholders in that company: While the manager possesses the ability (i.e., expertise), the shareholders hold the sovereignty and supervise the manager's activities in a general way. At another point, Sun uses the metaphor of a car owner and his chauffeur, stating, "The nation is a great automobile and the government officers are the great chauffeurs." The message throughout is the same: Trust the experts, replacing them only if they conclusively prove themselves untrustworthy.

Sun's interest in smooth administration does not imply a disinterest in checks and balances. On the contrary, he advocates a variety of mechanisms by which citizens can restrain excesses on the part of officials. Four mechanisms especially attract him: elections, initiatives, referendums, and the right of recall. All of these mechanisms work by majority rule. If the majority of voters support a particular candidate, they can place that person into office (election). If the majority supports the creation of a new law, they can propose it (initiative), while if the majority supports the abrogation of an existing law, they can vote to amend or eliminate it (referendum). Finally, if the majority is strongly dissatisfied with the actions of a particular official, they can remove that person from office before their term is completed (recall). Sun declares that all four of these mechanisms are employed in some states in the northwestern United States. Eager as always to absorb the best of what the world has to offer, Sun would like to see them adopted in a future China as well.

The political system that Sun advocates is a government comprised of five branches: legislative, executive, judicial, examinational, and censorial. The first three branches—legislative, executive, and judicial—are the same as the three main branches of government in the United States. In imperial China, these branches were combined together in the person of the emperor, who created, applied, and judged laws. Despite this apparent centralization of power, imperial China had its own system of checks and balances: Civil service examinations, rather than the emperor, selected talent for government service, while the censorate impeached corrupt officials and remonstrated with the emperor when he violated customary law. Accordingly, Sun wishes to combine the divisions of power present in the two systems by establishing both the three government branches of the United States *and* the two extra government branches of imperial China. The intent is to create a government that will be "the most complete and the finest in the world." The government of the Republic of China today utilizes this five-branch system, which in practice has often proved slow and unwieldy. In any case, Sun's advocacy of such a system once again demonstrates his insistence that China draw on its past as it moves into the future.

Sun does not hold that the political system he envisions can be foisted on the Chinese people all at once. Rather, there needs to be a period of transition between the old regime and the new one. More precisely, the shift to democracy should take place in three distinct stages. First, there needs to be a period of military rule in which the government suppresses counterrevolutionary forces (such as groups supporting the old dynastic system) throughout the nation. Once this is complete, a period of civic education will follow, in which expert guides teach the Chinese how to vote and perform other civic duties at the district level. Finally, when every district in China is functioning in accordance with the new system, a constitution can be announced and a national parliament elected. Sun was not consistent regarding how long the transitional periods ought to last. Indeed, one receives the overall impression that the government would be able to shorten or extend them based on its continuing assessment of conditions on the ground. In any event, the basic idea was plain enough: The Chinese people need political tutelage before they can be entrusted with their own sovereignty.

Given Sun's various modifications, how democratic is the Chinese-style "democracy" that he has outlined? It is hard to say, in part because he has not provided enough details. It is clear, however, that he feels both attracted to and repelled by democracy as the modern West has developed it. China scholar David Strand has captured these ambivalent feelings ably in his description of Sun's thought as "caught between a commitment to democracy undermined by hostility toward individual and group autonomy and a tendency toward authoritarian politics restrained by a romantic faith in a republic based on cultural consent." Neither Western-style democracy nor authoritarianism leaves Sun entirely comfortable, inasmuch as the former strikes him as too messy and the latter as too oppressive. Accordingly, he tried to combine elements of each, hoping and believing that he had arrived at a synthesis that could last far into the future.

The Principle of People's Livelihood

I have argued that for Sun Yatsen, everything comes back to nationalism. This is obvious in the case of the first principle—nationalism—which focuses directly on China's position in the world. It is also true for the second principle—democracy—which seeks to tap into the energies and loyalties of the Chinese people in a way that traditional monarchy never could. Surprisingly, at first, it is true as well for the third principle—people's livelihood—which aims to strengthen China by raising the standard of living of its people to world, and specifically Western, levels.

For well over half a century, the principle of people's livelihood has been highly controversial among Chinese and foreigners alike. The central issue is whether Sun Yatsen sought to introduce a socialist economic system into China. The answer to this ultimately depends on how one defines "socialism," a notoriously slippery term. If by socialism one means collective ownership of a society's means of producing and distributing goods, the answer has to be "no." If, however, one means government control over certain critical industries, taxation of other industries, and a degree of equalization of land ownership in the countryside, the answer will be "yes." Sun was a socialist of a very moderate sort who sought to utilize socialist policies as a means of allaying, rather than provoking, conflict between social classes.

Sun himself identified the principle of people's livelihood with socialism, and several times even with "communism." His sympathy with the plight of industrial workers was evidently first awakened during his 1896–1897 visit to London. Fittingly, the 1890s were a period in which socialist ideas and militant labor unions were especially prominent in Great Britain. There was little industry in China at that point, but Sun foresaw the possibility of future tension there too between capitalists and workers. He admired German Chancellor Otto von Bismarck's solution to the problem, which was to socialize certain industries and use their revenue to pacify the workers by establishing social programs for them. Interestingly, Sun's support for such a paternalistic approach is of a piece with his overall nationalism: The Chinese nation would be stronger, he consistently argued, if it were not riven with internal confrontations.

One reformist proposal that Sun particularly appreciated was the "single tax" advocated by American progressive **Henry George**. Henry George was one of a number of figures active in the United States and Great Britain during the late nineteenth and early twentieth centuries who sought a middle path between free market liberalism and revolutionary socialism. George himself had lived in California during an era in which throngs of settlers from further east were immigrating and driving land prices to astronomical levels. These enormous price increases struck him as a source of grave injustice: Landlords could make tremendous sums of money simply by renting out pieces of land without adding any improvements. This tended to remove the land—the ultimate source of wealth, in George's view—from productive use, thereby enriching the landlords at the expense of the rest of society. George's solution was simple: The government should collect the entire "unearned increment"—the entire price increase on unimproved land—as tax. This, he felt, would put an end to harmful land speculation while providing the government with enough money that it could abolish all other taxes. George's eloquent advocacy of this "single tax" plan brought him millions of readers and sustained public attention throughout the English-speaking world.

Sun supported George's plan, with a major caveat: Instead of taxing away all of the "unearned increment," he proposed to have landowners assess the value of their own land, after which the government would collect one percent of the value as tax. To ensure that landowners assessed their land accurately (rather than undervaluing it), he would give the government the right to purchase the land at its appraised value. Overall, Sun's version of the single tax was a good deal more moderate than that proposed by George. Despite this, it had the same purpose and even a similar origin: Sun and other Chinese were familiar with land speculation because sharp increases in land prices had jolted coastal China in much the same way they had coastal California.

Sun's interest in George's ideas is an example of his larger search for ways to avoid extreme disparities in wealth without harming individual initiative. Overall, however, he felt that the China of the early twentieth century was not yet afflicted with the sort of gap between rich and poor that pervaded the industrial West. As he sweepingly declared, "There is no especially rich class [in China], there is only a general poverty. The 'inequalities between rich and poor' which the Chinese speak of are only differences within the poor class . . ." Accordingly, his immediate priority was to generate wealth, utilizing government and private sector projects to lay railroad tracks, open mines, construct steamships, establish manufacturing industries, and mechanize agriculture for the purpose. China first needed to *have* wealth, after all, before any of that wealth could be distributed among the people of the country. As he stated in another book published in 1922, "it is my idea to *make capitalism create socialism in China* so that these two economic forces of human evolution will work side by side . . ." (emphasis added). Significantly, this is the approach that leaders of the **People's Republic of China** have championed since the 1980s, when the government abandoned hard-line Communism in favor of a tepid socialism that draws most of its vitality from the private sector.

In short, the principle of people's livelihood is a balancing act: Sun wants the government to take care of all Chinese without denying extra benefits to those who display extra initiative in the marketplace. One of the sayings by which he is best remembered is, "All under heaven belongs to the people." Applied to his economic views, however, this meant that all have the right to a share of China's future prosperity, not that all have the right to an *equal* share of that prosperity.

The Principles in Historical Perspective

Many Western writers have found the Three People's Principles less than over-whelmingly impressive. As the famed China scholar John King Fairbank flatly stated of Sun's expositions, "The writings he left are banal." Others have pointed to the many contradictions, inaccuracies, and ambiguities in Sun's explanations of the principles. Part of the problem is situational: Sun had to compose his lectures on the Three People's Principles hurriedly at a time when his health was beginning to fail. Yet that does not fully account for the tendentious quality of Sun's writing. Indeed, it often appears as if he adopts his political positions primarily for emotional reasons, weakly disguising this fact by marshaling strained arguments and slanted evidence to support himself. Sun is supposed to have been a gently impressive speaker, but it is the awkwardness of a good deal of his logic rather than his sincerity that comes across most on the printed page.

A related issue is that of how original Sun's ideas actually are. His emphasis on national unity and his paternalistic view of the state resemble similar motifs in Liang Qichao's famous writings at the beginning of the twentieth century. Moreover, the concept of a multifaceted program to boost "people's livelihood"—along with the term itself—was anticipated in Kang Youwei's 1895 written protest against the Treaty of Shimonoseki. Yet the larger point is less that Sun's ideas are somewhat derivative than that he shared the concerns of his transitional generation, which keenly experienced the attractions of both Chinese cultural tradition and Western military and economic success. These attractions led Sun, like Liang and Kang, to combine a quasi-Confucian expectation of government benevolence with a modern stress on efficiency and technological power. This combination, in turn, has attracted successive generations of Chinese, who have sought the reassurance of their cultural past even as they rush headlong into the future.

In global terms, Sun's Three People's Principles also carry an important reminder about the character of the modern nation-state. Nationalism, democracy, and people's livelihood all highlight the intense relationship that exists in modern nations between governments and the peoples over whom they rule. In each nation, the government owes its people a sense of participation (democracy or some other form of mobilization) and opportunities for sustenance and social justice (people's livelihood). The people, in turn, owe their government absolute loyalty, including a willingness to die in battle if necessary in order to protect the nation against external foes (nationalism). Sun Yatsen saw that this intense relationship, so central to successful modern nations, had been lacking in the China of old. He was determined that it would prevail in the China of the future.

In Pursuit of Revolution

While Sun Yatsen was envisioning China's future in the first decade of the twentieth century, China itself was experiencing an upsurge in modern nationalistic thought and activity. This latter was based on what China, and especially urban China, had experienced since the Opium War of 1839–1841. Let us recapitulate. The Opium War concluded with the Treaty of Nanjing, a one-sided treaty that began a protracted "Century of Humiliation" (1842–1943) at the hands of Western powers. In response to deteriorating conditions in south China, the Taiping Rebellion swept over much of the country in the 1850s and for a time threatened the very life of the Qing dynasty. Subsequently, the Self-Strengthening Movement of the Qing government attempted to improve China's international position through military and economic reforms. As the results of the Sino-French (1884) and Sino-Japanese (1894–1895) wars indicate, Self-Strengthening did not succeed on its own terms. Indeed, a scramble for concessions (1897–1898) among Western powers and Japan led to the rapid creation of foreign spheres of influence along parts of China's seacoast. Seeking to stem the tide, reformist Confucian scholars such as Kang Youwei and Liang Qichao advised Emperor Guangxu to institute extensive changes during the Hundred Days of Reform (1898). The movement ground to a halt, however, when the Empress Dowager Cixi and allied conservative forces persecuted the scholars and sequestered the emperor. Soon thereafter, the Boxer Uprising (1900), a popular nativistic movement aided by the Qing government, sought to repulse the foreigners once and for all but wound up bringing further humiliation to China. In this context, an aging Cixi reluctantly agreed to reorganize the Manchu-led Qing government along largely Western lines by means of the so-called New Policies.

The New Policies form the political backdrop for the deepening instability of China during the decade that followed the Boxer Rebellion. For a composite approach to this instability, it is helpful to turn briefly to *The Anatomy of Revolution*, a famous work by historian Crane Brinton that compares several modern Western revolutions to discern the pattern by which revolutions typically take place. Of special interest to us, Brinton describes the sorts of conditions that exist in a society as it heads toward a revolution. These conditions include the following: (1) the government is financially strapped and administratively inefficient; (2) social classes ranged near the top compete bitterly for power and recognition; (3) revolutionaries emerge, passionately arguing that present unjust circumstances can be changed; (4) intellectuals have transferred their allegiance to the cause of the revolutionaries; (5) the government's leadership has grown soft toward its opponents; and (6) the government's own military has been infiltrated by revolutionary ideas. It turns out that all of these conditions were present in Qing China during the first decade of the twentieth century.

Regarding the first of Brinton's conditions, the Qing government was impoverished by foreign claims on its revenues and hampered by its long history of inefficiency (as Sun pointed out in his 1894 letter to Li Hongzhang). Second, Chinese merchants and scholars alike were finding Manchu officials' pretensions increasingly intolerable as the decade proceeded. Third and fourth, revolutionaries such as Sun Yatsen were receiving a rapidly widening hearing among Chinese intellectuals for their view that China's problems could be resolved through a revolution against the Qing dynasty. Fifth, the Qing government had largely scrapped its traditional system of governance and was uncertain how much ground it should yield to its angry opponents. Finally and most damningly, the New Army created by the New Policies became heavily infiltrated by secret society members sympathetic to the revolutionary cause.

The overall picture that emerges of the Qing dynasty's last decade is of a government that was on the defensive—clumsy and unsure of itself—and of a revolutionary force that was on the *offensive*—backed by an expanding array of thinkers and soldiers who were convinced that the Qing government alone was preventing the re-emergence of China as a central force in world affairs. In light of this dynamic, it would have been very difficult for any government— even one far more united and capable than the Qing—to have successfully implemented drastic changes without prompting a severe backlash against its rule. As another incisive student of politics, Alexis de Tocqueville, once remarked, "the most dangerous moment for a bad government is usually when it begins to reform itself."

Revolutionaries versus Reformists

If the Qing government was having difficulty consolidating itself for the coming struggle, opponents of the government were equally split. The two types of opponents, clashing repeatedly during the post-Boxer decade, were the revolutionaries and the reformists. Revolutionaries such as Sun Yatsen aimed for a straightforward overthrow of the Qing dynasty and its replacement by a republic. Reformists such as Kang Youwei and Liang Qichao were harder to pin down: While they invariably demanded that Cixi release Emperor Guangxu, they were less clear on what should happen next. Based on their writings, they appeared to want Emperor Guangxu to institute a set of reforms that would go beyond those of the New Policies. These reforms would refashion China's government as a constitutional monarchy complete with a parliament and elections for public office. In addition, reformists sometimes left open the possibility that in the very long run, China could become a democracy with an elected president. For the time being, however, they wanted some version of the Qing dynasty to continue.

The organization that promoted reformist aspirations was the **Emperor Protection Society**, which Kang Youwei founded in Canada in 1899. Its leading propagandist was Liang Qichao, who had grown disgusted with Sun's insistence on rapid political upheaval. Liang, an ardent gradualist, felt that overthrowing the Manchus would lead to unnecessary chaos and tempt the Western powers to partition China among themselves. It was far better, he believed, for China's current government to oversee the radical changes that China had to make for its survival.

Liang was very successful at spreading his reformist message on the Hawaiian Islands during his visit there in 1899. He completely marginalized Sun's Revive China Society—even to the point of converting Sun's brother Sun Mei to the reformist cause! As the revolutionaries were victorious in the long run, it can be tempting to minimize this reformist challenge. Yet at the beginning of the twentieth century, its attraction was great and Sun and other revolutionaries had to struggle persistently against it to gain the upper hand. The reformist position featured a royal in distress—the sequestered Emperor Guangxu—and maintained that by rescuing the emperor from Cixi's control, China could successfully modernize and Chinese people around the world could gain the respect they deserved. In such a view, the allure of royalty and the urgency of modernization subtly interfused, yielding an appeal that was difficult to resist.

When Sun visited Hawaii in 1903, he set out to win over Hawaiian Chinese who had embraced the reformist message. He did so, first, by turning a Chinese-language newspaper, *The Hawaiian Chinese News*, into a mouthpiece for the revolutionary cause. He personally wrote articles for the paper, attacking inconsistencies in the reformist perspective. For example, the reformists claimed that they sought "revolution" for China, even as they desired to shelter the emperor from the impact of such revolution. Sun took direct aim at this contradiction: "Liang is a man with two ways of talking, like a rat looking both ways. If his revolutionary talk is sincere, then his 'emperor-protection' talk must be spurious. If his 'emperor-protection' talk is sincere, then his revolutionary utterances must be false." Sun also argued that far from protecting China from partition, Manchu leaders had signed agreements with Western powers that gave the latter control over pieces of Chinese territory and fed the Western appetite for still more.

Sun now embraced propaganda in its various forms. For example, he gave public lectures before hundreds of ordinary Hawaiian Chinese in the cities of Hilo and Honolulu. While Sun was doubtlessly watched by Qing government agents at these events, the agents were no longer as aggressive as they had been in the preceding century, having already lost control over the Hawaiian Chinese community to anti-Cixi reformists. Consequently, Sun was able to appeal broadly to Hawaii's Chinese for funds for future insurrections. As it turns out, these funds would be vital: Although Sun's brother soon reconverted to the revolutionary side, new American land regulations had reduced his wealth to the point that he could no longer help finance Sun's radical activities.

Sun also began to broaden his propagandizing and fund-raising far beyond Japan and Hawaii. Indeed, by 1904, his organization had four newspapers—one apiece in Hawaii, Hong Kong, Singapore, and San Francisco. This was not yet as many as the reformists controlled, but he was gaining on them. In addition, he distributed a pamphlet in New York City titled *The True Solution of the Chinese Question* that aimed to arouse the sympathies of Americans in general. The pamphlet laid out Sun's case against the Manchus, presenting the latter as the despoilers of Chinese civilization. Anticipating Western concerns, it addressed the issue of the "yellow peril"—that is, the belief among a number of Caucasian Americans that a strong China would menace the Western world. Pointing to the many opportunities for trade between a modernized China and the United States, Sun maintained instead that "the yellow peril may after all be changed into the yellow blessing." He concluded the pamphlet by harkening back to the United States' own revolutionary experience, declaring, "We hope we may find many Lafayettes among you." Sun had evidently retained his keen sense as to how to appeal to the unconvinced.

As the decade progressed and the Revolutionary Alliance took shape, Sun extended his organizational activities to wherever Chinese communities existed and reformists had a foothold. For all his persistence, however, his reformist opponents long maintained an organizational advantage: They understood far better than he did how important it was to use organizers whom local Chinese communities respected and to have those organizers join existing organizations in order to influence them from within. Sun could occasionally be savvy on this score, joining the North American branch of the Triads in 1904 in order to bring it over to his side. Nevertheless, his usual approach was to seek out individuals to whom he could transmit a part of his own fervor, regardless of whether those individuals had either community prestige or organizational skills. This preference for mobilization over organization would continue to limit the global expansion of the Revolutionary Alliance until the reformists ran aground late in the decade for reasons that we will explore later in this chapter.

The French Connection

We have already seen that Sun's Revolutionary Alliance first took shape as a combination of his Revive China Society with several similar groups, including Huang Xing's China Arise Society. Song Jiaoren, a prominent member of the China Arise Society, had founded *Twentieth-Century China* as the Society's mouthpiece. With the creation of the Revolutionary Alliance, it was renamed *The People's Journal* and established as the flagship newspaper of the new organization. The famous scholar-revolutionary Zhang Binglin became its editor and he and several other highly talented writers tirelessly churned out essays for the paper arguing for revolution and against the New Policies and the reformists.

For his part, Sun left Japan for Saigon in French Indochina even before *The People's Journal* was fully underway. Indeed, he spent much of the next three years in Indochina cementing close relations with local French imperialists and using their assistance to arrange a series of insurrections in southern China. In some respects, Sun had abandoned the organization he had just created—and still officially led—in order to pursue his own dream of provoking a revolution with foreign support. Odd as this may appear, it typified his overall outlook toward organizations. In the view of Marie-Claire Bergère, Sun believed that "an institution has no existence without whoever embodies it," which in the case of the Revolutionary Alliance "happened to be himself." Thus, he surrounded himself with several Cantonese students from Japan—men whom he groomed as his personal followers—while he undertook his conspiracies in Indochina. He also had the military-minded Huang Xing serve as the leader of his southern Chinese insurrections. As to the rest of the Revolutionary Alliance, he spent its money and otherwise left it to fare as best it could without him.

The area on which Sun and the French imperialists concentrated their efforts consisted of several southern Chinese provinces—including resource-rich Yunnan—that directly abutted French Indochina. The area was mountainous and populated by all manner of bandits. While it fell under loose Chinese control, the presence of so many bandits suggested that its national affiliation could easily shift. Some French imperialists in Indochina dreamed of adding the area to Indochina itself, which would give them access to Yunnan's minerals and perhaps to the thriving trade of nearby Sichuan as well. A railway already linked the Indochinese city of Hanoi with Yunnan, and there was always the possibility that extending the railway and acquiring nearby territory could prove to be a windfall to the French imperialists. Sun encouraged French authorities to think along these lines, promising them that if his rebels were able to create a separate state in south China, the French would receive extensive economic benefits in it. This was highly ironic, given that Sun's Revolutionary Alliance angrily condemned the impact of Western imperialism on China. Sun, however, believed that his goal—the creation of a revolutionary government in even a part of China—justified the proimperialist methods he used to achieve it.

Hagiographers in both mainland China and Taiwan happily attribute the six small-scale insurrections that followed during 1906–1908 to Sun's leadership. In fact, however, Huang Xing played an indispensable role, conferring extensively with local bandit leaders to coordinate their activities. Of the six insurrections, the most important—and the only one in which Sun personally participated—took place in 1907 at a large mountain pass in Guangxi province named Zhennanguan. While several hundred Qing troops guarded this pass, many of them supported the revolutionary cause, displaying little resistance as Sun's band of rebels overtook them. Despite this initial success, it rapidly became clear that movement beyond the immediate area would be difficult: The Qing arsenal at the pass had few weapons and loyal Qing troops a distance away were in a position to fire at the rebels. Indeed, a week later a Qing counterattack retook the pass and the operation ended. This insurrection, limited as it was, marked the only time between late 1895 and the revolution of 1911 that Sun set foot—albeit illicitly—on Chinese soil.

As one failed insurrection followed another, the attitude of the French Indochinese government toward Sun's activities gradually soured. The French government in Paris had already shifted its attention away from imperialist expansion and toward European affairs. Meanwhile, the Indochinese government saw that the Qing dynasty maintained effective control over its territory, which prompted it to seek friendly relations with the dynasty rather than provoke it needlessly by assisting Sun Yatsen. The net result was that Indochina expelled Sun and his coconspirators in 1908.

Despite this anticlimactic denouement, Sun Yatsen's cooperation with France highlights several important components of his revolutionary strategy. First, he depended abjectly on foreign aid. This remained the case throughout his adult life: In contrast to many of his revolutionary peers, he consistently believed that foreign assistance was essential to any effort to revitalize China. Second, he and Huang Xing actively sought to infiltrate the New Army. Although they had not yet achieved much success on this score, they would begin to fare better by the end of the decade. Finally, Sun's efforts to create a separate state in the south foreshadowed the "southern strategy" that would dominate the final decade of his life. Like earlier generations of Chinese rebels, Sun sought to make the most of his marginality by consolidating an area along an edge of China as his power-base. From that remote base, he felt, his supporters would be ideally situated to launch attacks against the center of power in Beijing.

Qing Efforts at Reform

As the first decade of the twentieth century continued, the Manchu government steadily accelerated its implementation of the New Policies. One major force behind this acceleration was **Yuan Shikai,** the most powerful ethnic Chinese in the history of the Qing dynasty. Yuan was the commander of the New Army of north China, which he reorganized as the Beiyang (literally, "Northern Ocean") Army. We need to become acquainted with him because he would come to play a critical role in both Sun's life and China's history during the 1910s.

Born into a family of Qing officials, Yuan Shikai moved upward through the military ranks in his youth. In the mid-1880s, Li Hongzhang appointed him as the Chinese representative to Korea, in which capacity he helped cause the Sino-Japanese War by advising Li to dispatch Chinese troops there. After a major role in the war itself, he was placed in charge of organizing a modern military force—the future Beiyang Army—for the Qing government. When Li Hongzhang died in 1901, Yuan assumed his functions by having himself appointed to Li's posts and by maintaining Li's close political relationship with Cixi. As leader of the Beiyang Army, Yuan steadily built up a force of 60,000 modern-trained soldiers that became the model for smaller military units elsewhere in China.

While Yuan focused on strengthening his army, the Qing government turned its attention to the creation of a modern constitution. This new constitution, based largely on that of Meiji Japan, would have a distinctly authoritarian tenor. Nevertheless, it did stipulate the gradual establishment of provincial assemblies, which were conceived as advisory bodies. In 1909, the members of these assemblies were selected through elections with limited male suffrage—the first elections in all of Chinese history. When the assemblies actually met, they quickly displayed an appetite for power, issuing a volley of petitions at the central Qing government. Such behavior typifies the increasing assertiveness of the provincial Chinese elites in the face of the various New Policies. Unnerved, the Qing government intermittently sought to constrain the elites with Manchu oversight, but this merely ensured that their confidence would be laced with feelings of urgency and resentment. Slowly but relentlessly, the elites wore down every new obstacle that the Qing government attempted to place in their way.

Sun Yatsen's Second Wind

Even as events began to slip beyond the control of the Qing government, Sun Yatsen was experiencing his own difficulties as leader of the Revolutionary Alliance. The first problem was that countries continued to expel him from their borders! Back in 1895, China had expelled him after his first failed Guangzhou Uprising and British Hong Kong had immediately followed suit. As we saw in Chapter 4, Sun's response was to take refuge in Japan, which became the center of his operations. In early 1907, however, Sun gave an incendiary public speech at Waseda University in Tokyo. Following the speech, the Qing government pressured the Japanese government into expelling him and not allowing him to return. As we have seen, French Indochina expelled him the following year. After he moved his operations further south, to British Singapore and British Malaya, he again alarmed local authorities, causing those colonial possessions, too, to expel him in 1910. By early 1911, there were few countries in East or Southeast Asia that would permit Sun to enter their territory. He was a wanted man—or at least, an *un*wanted man—nearly everywhere.

The circumstances that surrounded Sun's expulsion from Japan caused special problems within his organization. To soften the impact of expulsion, the Japanese government had quietly given Sun a good deal of money. Sun accepted the money without consulting other figures in the Revolutionary Alliance and spent it on weapons for yet another insurrection in south China. When this came to light, it brought the many simmering tensions within the Alliance to a head. *The People's Journal* editor Zhang Binglin bitterly accused Sun of wasting the money on luxuries rather than leaving it for the Alliance newspaper. Zhang and others argued that Sun's behavior as their president was secretive, rigid, and overbearing, and many Alliance members—especially those from central China—began to push for his removal from office. In a sign of how serious the rift had become, one figure from the Alliance even traveled to various Southeast Asian Chinese communities and encouraged people *not* to contribute when Sun came to raise money.

The Revolutionary Alliance was clearly in trouble. What saved it from disintegrating completely was the relationship between Sun Yatsen and Huang Xing, his vice president. Although Sun and Huang, too, sometimes clashed, Huang refused to back Zhang's demand for Sun's ouster. Indeed, Huang's continued support for Sun's leadership made him the bridge between the two major groups within the Alliance: the central Chinese (which included Huang) and the southern Chinese (which included Sun). The central Chinese members were typically scholars from elite lineages, and as such they supported insurrections against the Qing government in central China, closer to the center of power. The southern Chinese members, on the other hand, continued to favor Sun's southern strategy even though it repeatedly failed to produce results. Huang's support enabled Sun to maintain his strategy, but the gulf between the two sides remained deep.

Following his expulsions from Japan and French Indochina, Sun moved his fund-raising operations far into Southeast Asia, to the Chinese communities of Singapore and Penang. As Western imperialism penetrated this region, ethnic Chinese came to hold a special position as middlemen between Western colonial administrations and local populations. In this position, a minority of Chinese had become very wealthy, and as such they became targets for the fund-raising efforts of revolutionaries and reformists alike. Indeed, of the 24 branches that the Revolutionary Alliance had established worldwide by the time of the 1911 revolution, 11—nearly half—were located in Southeast Asia. The Alliance under Sun spread its revolutionary message in the region through a variety of media, including newspapers, drama troupes, and reading clubs (quasi-libraries that made Chinese-language materials available to those too poor to afford them). Southeast Asia's ethnic Chinese responded to the Alliance's efforts positively and generously, prompting Sun in later years to call overseas Chinese the "mother of the revolution."

Despite its internal rifts, then, the Revolutionary Alliance was gaining popularity among ethnic Chinese in Southeast Asia and elsewhere. In contrast, the rival Emperor Protection Society had run into grave problems. In accordance with the wishes of Canadian Chinese followers, Kang Youwei had permitted the Society to be turned into a commercial operation with investments on several continents. Many of these investments, profitable at first, eventually turned sour, especially when the Mexican Revolution of 1910 drastically reduced the value of the Society's extensive real-estate holdings there. Meanwhile, Kang was spending considerable amounts of money on cruises with a 17-year-old female consort to such exotic locales as Pompeii, Copenhagen, and Monte Carlo. Increasingly, Kang came to be seen as eccentric and outlandish, even by his own followers. Moreover, when Emperor Guangxu died in 1908, the Emperor Protection Society had, strictly speaking, no distressed emperor left to "protect." The group recast itself as the National Constitution Society, but nothing helped it recover the popularity it had enjoyed earlier.

While the reformists foundered, Sun's efforts to enlist foreign support led him in an unexpected direction: American adventurer Homer Lea. Lea was an intense, well-educated young man with several physical deformities—notably a hunched back—and an acute interest in world military affairs. Lea focused especially on East Asian developments, achieving fame for a book he wrote that predicted future conflict with Japan. Significantly for us, his far more positive view of China led him during the first several years of the twentieth century to support the Emperor Protection Society. To assist the Society, he trained militias in several American Chinatowns for possible future use in liberating China from its conservative government. Over time, however, Lea grew dissatisfied with the Society's underlying Confucianism and its financial corruption. He shifted his loyalty to the

Revolutionary Alliance, at which point he and Sun swiftly set to work plotting a change of regime for Qing China.

The plan they drew up was simple—and completely unrealistic. Sun and Lea would cooperate with Lea's friend Charles Boothe, a retired banker with wealthy contacts, to raise $10,000,000 to buy weapons and ship them to Guangdong province. Lea would lead a group of mercenary officers to train a revolutionary army in south China, which, at the appropriate time, would use the stored weapons to overthrow the Qing government. Following the success of the revolution, Americans who had donated money for the weapons would receive hefty economic privileges in China's reconstruction. None of this actually happened, of course: Boothe never even raised any money for the scheme. Despite this, the link between Sun and Lea—which remained strong right up to Lea's death in 1912—showed the lengths Sun was willing to go to in order to raise money and attract supporters for his revolution.

During the first decade of the twentieth century, Sun Yatsen utilized a wide range of methods to oppose the Qing dynasty and the reformists. Certain methods, such as his concentrated use of propaganda against the reformists, proved effective. Other methods, such as his military cooperation with French imperialists in Indochina, were at least realistic. In a number of cases, however, Sun behaved unwisely, neglecting effective organization within overseas Chinese communities, provoking needless conflict within his Revolutionary Alliance, and hatching implausible plots with foreign adventurers. Later generations of Chinese have almost universally forgiven these lapses in judgment—when they have even noticed them—because they have respected the underlying sense of impatience that brought them about. That impatience, which would last through the remainder of Sun's life, comprised his desire to create a newer China.

In any event, while Sun was critical in fashioning an anti-Qing climate of opinion in Chinese communities both outside and inside China, he did not deliver the sharpest blow against the Qing dynasty in the short term. Rather, what landed that blow was the twin deaths of the Empress Dowager Cixi and Emperor Guangxu in late 1908. Guangxu died a day before Cixi, despite his relative youth—he was 37—and prior good health. This has led most historians to conclude that when Cixi realized she would die, she first had Guangxu poisoned to avenge his youthful defiance during the Hundred Days of Reform. Whatever the case, with both Cixi and Guangxu dead, the chances for vigorous leadership of the Qing government were now eliminated. The new emperor was Xuantong—better known as Puyi—who was the two-and-a-half-year-old son of Guangxu's brother, Prince Chun. Prince Chun, corrupt and indecisive, would act as the main regent for his son. To Sun and his fellow revolutionaries, a new door appeared to be opening.

8

The News in Denver

By the end of the first decade of the twentieth century, it was clear to all observers that the Qing government was heavily weakened by domestic and international circumstances alike. Teetering on the edge, it would collapse altogether in 1911. Ironically, when this collapse—which happened in a fashion no one could possibly have predicted—took place, Sun Yatsen was not anywhere near China but was instead traveling within the United States. Marie-Claire Bergère refers to this as his "missed appointment with history." This may be an overstatement: Sun soon returned to China and took charge of a revolutionary government created to replace the Qing dynasty. Nevertheless, his victory was distinctly bittersweet for reasons that this chapter and the next one will make clear.

With the deaths of Emperor Guangxu and the Empress Dowager Cixi in 1908, the Qing government became virtually rudderless. Prince Chun, regent for the child emperor Puyi, intensely disliked Yuan Shikai, whom he regarded as the betrayer of his brother Guangxu. Consequently, he removed Yuan from his government positions in early 1909. In practice, this meant that Prince Chun would have to contend with restive provincial elites and soldiers-turned-revolutionaries on his own.

He did not have to wait for long. In 1910 and 1911, China was racked by a series of natural disasters, including horrific flooding along the Yangzi River. As natural disasters traditionally signified that heaven was withdrawing its support for the ruling dynasty, civil disturbances were rife. Alongside the spontaneous disturbances, the Revolutionary Alliance attempted an uprising in Guangzhou in February 1910, focusing its efforts on New Army soldiers there who mutinied against the government. The mutiny was soon contained, but the Alliance quickly began to plan yet another uprising concentrated on Guangzhou.

In November 1910, the Revolutionary Alliance held a conference in Penang, Malaya, at which it coordinated plans for the next revolt in Guangzhou. The idea was similar to that of the 1895 uprising: Outside commandos (called "dare-to-dies") would assist groups revolting within the city. Huang Xing, in overall charge of the operation, made sure that everyone was adequately armed by having weapons smuggled into the city in curtained sedan chairs that were supposed to contain wedding brides. Rumors proliferated—as they often do in a tight-knit society like China's—and the government brought in reinforcements. At the actual uprising, a rebel force heavy with New Army troops set the governor-general's headquarters on fire. Nevertheless, the resulting state of confusion worked to the advantage of the government, which was able to restore order even before the Alliance's commandos could reach the city. As a sign of its determination, the government executed 86 people associated with the revolt. Revolutionaries, in turn, managed to retrieve the bodies of 72 of these people and buried them together. Extensively commemorated after the fall of the Qing government, these "72 martyrs" continue to receive homage even today in the pages of school textbooks throughout the Chinese-speaking world.

The failure of the Guangzhou Uprising—regarded by Sun Yatsen as his tenth insurrection—was a heavy blow for the Revolutionary Alliance, which had spent more money on this revolt than on any of the others. Nevertheless, the central role played by New Army soldiers in the uprising showed, again, that the army was rife with soldiers who regarded it as their patriotic duty to oppose their government rather than to support it.

Running Off the Track

Railroads play a critical role in the fall of the Qing dynasty. Historically, the latter half of the nineteenth century featured rapid rail expansion worldwide. Railroads were initially disfavored in China, however, as ancestral graves were thickly scattered through peasants' fields and it was considered disrespectful to build over or relocate them. These qualms held less weight following the scramble for concessions in the 1890s as Western investors began to build lines through their nations' spheres of influence to exploit their economic potential.

The single longest and most important railroad in early twentieth-century China was the line that connected Beijing in the northeast to Wuhan, a bustling metropolis along the Yangzi River in central China. Before this line was completed in 1905, negotiations were already underway to extend it, with one line linking Wuhan to Guangzhou in the south and another linking it to Sichuan province further west. The Qing government promised that the people of the affected provinces could build and finance the lines themselves, in contrast to the lines that foreigners were building at the same time.

Funding from the affected provinces proved inadequate. To take up the slack, the Qing government announced on May 9, 1911, that it would "nationalize" the main rail lines in China, meaning that in the future it would accept responsibility for subsidizing and collecting profits from these lines. Eleven days later, the government signed a contract with a multinational banking consortium for a large loan that used the rights to government railways as collateral. Taken together, these two actions gave provincial elites a terrible impression regarding the Qing government's intentions: It appeared as though the government was taking the rail lines away from the provincial elites only in order to resell them to foreigners! Actually, the government's primary aim was to expedite the construction of rail lines that had stalled for lack of local funds. In the prevailing atmosphere of suspicion vis-à-vis the central government, however, the actions seemed to fulfill the revolutionaries' long-standing claim that Manchus and Westerners were conspiring to harm Chinese interests.

A large-scale campaign calling itself the Railway Protection Movement quickly materialized to buy back the rights to the rail lines from the Qing government. The government tried to calm the waters by promising compensation to investors whose lines it planned to nationalize, but the rates of compensation it offered to investors in Sichuan province were much lower than those it was offering elsewhere. The result was that the Railway Protection Movement became increasingly strident in Sichuan, featuring emotional rallies and strikes there.

There is a Chinese saying that Sichuan—large, baking-hot, and fiercely independent—is invariably the first province to break away from a nationwide Chinese government and the last to rejoin it. As demonstrations continued there in early September, the Qing government moved to suppress them, killing 32 people at a large rally in Chengdu, the provincial capital. The "Chengdu Massacre," as it was dubbed, functioned somewhat as the Boston Massacre had in the American Revolution: In both cases, a government intent on order instead managed to convince bystanders that it no longer deserved their respect. Henceforth, conditions in Sichuan rapidly deteriorated. To restore control, the government was compelled to transport large numbers of New Army troops from Wuhan in neighboring Hubei province.

The emergency transfer of so many troops unwittingly paved the way for the revolution that overthrew the Qing dynasty. This revolution, which Sun Yatsen had been promoting abroad for the previous 16 years, began on October 10, 1911—nicknamed "Double Ten" in Chinese. And the place where it started was none other than Wuhan.

Lying at the confluence of the Yangzi and Han rivers, Wuhan is comprised of three adjacent cities known as Hankou, Hanyang, and Wuchang, respectively. Both in 1911 and today, the combined metropolis of Wuhan forms one of the great industrial centers of China as a whole. Within the metropolis, Wuchang stood out in 1911 as a center of weapons production even as it also harbored numerous revolutionaries among its New Army forces. Indeed, the Revolutionary Alliance maintained contact with some of these revolutionaries and was apprised of their plans to stage an insurrection in late October.

The actual revolution began by accident. Hankou, a port opened to preferential Western trade by treaty, contained an area called the Russian Concession in which Russian law prevailed. Local revolutionaries meeting at their headquarters in the Concession were making bombs on October 9 when one bomb accidentally exploded. The sheer size of the explosion attracted local Qing investigators, who discovered membership registers at the site for local revolutionary groups. Acting quickly to avoid prosecution, New Army soldiers in Wuchang revolted on the morning of October 10 by storming Wuchang's main forts. With loyal troops in short supply, the Manchu governor-general and the Chinese army commander of Hubei responded by fleeing the city.

Over the course of the next two days, troops in Hanyang and Hankou joined the rebels and established a military government for Hubei province with brigade commander Li Yuanhong as their leader. Li balked at first, and indeed, it is alleged that soldiers held a gun to his head and asked him whether he would prefer to become the George Washington of China or to die on the spot! In any case, he agreed, giving the revolutionaries the cover of a figure whom Hubei elites and local foreigners alike respected.

On October 12, the new Hubei military government sent proclamations to China's various provinces urging them to join the revolt. After 10 days in which provinces took a wait-and-see attitude, the first secessions appeared—beginning, of course, with Sichuan. The trend quickly accelerated, and by late November, fully two-thirds of the provinces of China—including nearly all of those south of the Great Wall—had withdrawn from the Qing dynasty.

The man whom many Chinese and foreigners turned to while these surreal events were unfolding was not Sun Yatsen but Yuan Shikai. Prince Chun's hatred for Yuan did not prevent him from asking Yuan to return to government service now that the dynasty was on the verge of collapse. Yuan, however, hedged his bets, demanding as the price for his return that the government place him in charge of all military forces, create a national assembly, and extend amnesty to all republican revolutionaries. Yuan received everything he sought and was named prime minister in early November. In that capacity, he quickly removed Manchus from positions of genuine power, replacing them with his followers in the Beiyang Army. For the time being, he allowed the child emperor Puyi to remain on the throne.

Having taken control over what remained of the Qing dynasty, Yuan began to place pressure on the revolutionaries. Both Yuan and the revolutionaries knew that the revolutionary side could not defeat the Beiyang Army. Yuan now set out to show the revolutionaries that he was willing to use this army against them: In the course of November, Yuan's forces reconquered Hankou and Hanyang, respectively. These bloody battles made it very clear to the revolutionaries that they would have to give Yuan at least some of what he wanted. At the same time, the revolutionaries also possessed a degree of leverage against Yuan: His troops could not prevent the city of Nanjing from falling into the revolutionaries' hands in early December and becoming their capital. Behind these specific battles, the broad situation that was taking shape was that north China lay under Yuan's control, while south China lay under the revolutionaries' control. If this standoff was to be resolved and China was to be reunited, someone would have to bring the two sides together and broker an agreement.

Where Was Sun?

One of the most popular tourist sites in Wuhan today is a large red-brick building that the Hubei military government used as its headquarters in October 1911 after the **Wuchang Uprising**. Visitors approaching this building first pass through a handsome public square, at the center of which stands a sizable copper statue of Sun Yatsen wearing a traditional Chinese scholar's dress and holding a Western top hat in one hand. In actual fact, however, Sun Yatsen never visited the Hubei military government during its short period as the storm center of the revolution against the Qing dynasty. Where was Sun, then?

He was in the United States doing what he had been doing for most of the preceding 16 years: raising money for the revolution. Expelled from virtually all of East Asia, he had left Asia in December 1910, arriving in Europe the same month. After a brief stay there, he sailed across the Atlantic to New York City and spent most of 1911 in major American cities, canvassing Chinese communities as usual.

Sun Yatsen was in Denver, Colorado, on October 11—a day after the Wuchang Uprising—when he finally read a week-old coded telegram from Huang Xing asking for funds for a prospective uprising in Hubei province. The following morning Sun had boarded a train for Kansas City and was perusing the morning newspaper when he read, to his great surprise, that the uprising had already taken place. Nor was this all: As he continued to travel by rail toward Chicago, he passed through St. Louis on October 14. An article in a newspaper he read there reported that if the emerging revolution in China succeeded, there were plans to have "Dr. Sun Yat-sen" serve as the republic's new president!

In short, Sun was halfway across the world as the revolution he had tirelessly promoted was unfolding. With his dream rapidly coming true, he had to decide what to do next. Upon thinking the matter through, he determined that rather than return to China right away, he would travel to Europe. There he could meet with Western European leaders and seek promises from them that they would remain neutral in the coming struggle between the Qing dynasty and the revolutionaries. Indeed, this is what he did, arriving in London, England, on October 20. Sun quickly contacted the British Foreign Office and received assurance of its neutrality. He noticed, however, that British officials regarded Yuan Shikai—more than the revolutionaries—as the most promising source of stability for China.

Sun next proceeded to Paris, where he met with French Prime Minister Georges Clemenceau. In France, too, he received a standard assurance of neutrality, although as in Great Britain he was unable to attract any loans for the revolutionary government. In any case, he felt reassured that European governments correctly understood the revolutionaries' aims and were not confusing them with those of the antiforeign Boxers of 11 years earlier.

Having accomplished what he could in Europe, Sun left it in late November as the impasse deepened between Yuan Shikai in northern China and the revolutionaries in the south. He reached Shanghai on Christmas day and received a warm welcome there. Earlier in December, delegates from the many secessionist provinces met in Nanjing and attempted to elect a president for themselves. They do not appear to have been waiting for Sun's return. Nevertheless, they found themselves deadlocked between a Wuchang-based faction that supported Li Yuanhong and a Shanghai-based faction that supported Huang Xing. Thus, when Sun did return to China, a movement quickly materialized that favored him as a compromise candidate between the two factions. The movement succeeded and Sun Yatsen was formally elected as Provisional President of the **Republic of China** on December 29, 1911.

Sun as Provisional President

Sun Yatsen spent a total of three months—January 1, 1912 to April 1, 1912—as the highest-ranking figure in the country to which he devoted his adult life. He ruled throughout this period from Nanjing, which had served as China's capital during the Ming dynasty (1369–1644) that directly preceded the Qing. The Ming dynasty itself had followed a century of Mongol rule over China and Ming Taizi, founder of the Ming dynasty, was greatly respected by secret society members and other Chinese as the figure who had restored native Chinese rule. Ming Taizi's tomb was located on Purple Mountain just outside Nanjing. On January 1, 1912, Sun made the highly symbolic gesture of having himself inaugurated at the tomb site as his way of promising that he would wrest rule over China from the Manchus just as Ming Taizi had wrested rule over China from the Mongols.

Sun located the headquarters for the new government in the office complex of the preceding Manchu governor-general. This complex—renamed the Presidential Palace—was to become a magnet for powerful governments in early twentieth-century China: The Nationalist government later ruled from it between 1927 and 1937, and a Japanese puppet government over eastern China ruled from it during World War II. As political power in China gyrated over succeeding decades among a dizzying variety of individuals and groups, it frequently sought to house itself in this complex first selected by Sun Yatsen.

Since mid-December, Yuan Shikai's northern government and the revolutionary southern government had been negotiating terms for a resolution to their impasse. The revolutionaries even offered the presidency of China to Yuan if he would recognize the southern government as the legitimate government over China. So far, Yuan had rejected this, leading to the election of Sun in December. Sun nevertheless believed that Yuan would eventually become president. Indeed, on the very day of his inauguration, Sun sent Yuan a telegram that read as follows: "Although I have accepted this position, for the time being, it is actually waiting for you, and my offer will eventually be made clear to the world. I hope that you will soon decide to accept this offer." Both then and later, Sun's decision to offer his position to Yuan Shikai rather than seek a lengthy presidency for himself was controversial. Sun, however, had focused his attention on the fact that Yuan controlled the strongest army in China and that any effort to dislodge him could invite both civil war and foreign intervention.

As Sun's period as president was brief, it is difficult to characterize his tenure in office. Overall, however, his record was mixed. On the one hand, he took certain important steps, such as prohibiting footbinding among women, mandating the cutting of men's queues, and amassing foreign loans to pay his soldiers and relieve regional famine. On the other hand, Sun's manner of governance tended to be chaotic. He appointed a cabinet—but he did not try to persuade its members to work together. He ruled alongside a parliament—but he often acted on his own authority without consulting it. In the meantime, overseas Chinese supporters and Japanese businessmen appeared at the Palace in droves seeking favors. In general, Sun's approach was highly secretive, as though he was still leading an underground organization. Like rebels-turned-leaders in many parts of the world, he found the transition from conspirator to statesman a very difficult one to make.

The largest issue that hung over Sun's presidency was that of how the north/south impasse would work itself out. The negotiations over the issue were especially intricate because in actuality *three* parties were involved: the Qing imperial family, Yuan Shikai, and the revolutionary government. The imperial family hoped that it could retain a degree of power as China entered the future. The revolutionary government, on the other hand, was vehemently anti-Manchu and sought to abolish the monarchical system completely. Yuan Shikai probably did not care one way or the other, but he would offer each side a degree of support for its objectives—in return for concessions to him.

The deal that the three parties eventually worked out took the form of an elaborate time line that all of the parties would obey. The time line ran as follows: First, Puyi would abdicate; second, Yuan would declare his support for a republic; third, Sun would resign his office; fourth, the parliament in Nanjing would elect Yuan as provisional president; fifth, Yuan would pledge to honor the constitution that the parliament was preparing; and finally, Yuan would be handed over the military power of the revolutionary government. The first item, Puyi's abdication, took place on February 12, 1912, and officially brought the Qing dynasty to an end after 268 years in power.

Items two and three—Yuan's declaration and Sun's resignation—quickly followed. Sun attached a special condition to his resignation, however: He charged that Yuan would have to come to Nanjing and accept it as the republic's long-term capital before he could receive full power over the government. After the Nanjing parliament elected Yuan as the republic's second provisional president (item four), it dispatched a delegation to Beijing to escort Yuan south to Nanjing. Yuan, however, wanted to stay in the north, where his power base lay. He instigated riots in Beijing while the southern delegation was in the city and then argued that he needed to remain in the north to maintain order there. Bowing to Yuan's power play, the delegation—and Sun in Nanjing—very reluctantly accepted Yuan's preference for Beijing as the capital.

Following Yuan's inauguration in Beijing on March 10, he pledged his support for the parliament's new constitution, which was duly promulgated (item five). Sun had originally supported an American style president-centered system for the Chinese republic. When it became clear that Yuan would become president, however, he and other revolutionaries shifted to prefer a British style "responsible cabinet" system that would place greater limits on presidential power. The constitution that the parliament actually drafted was an awkward compromise between these two positions that left the relationship between the president and the cabinet dangerously unclear.

The last part of the agreed-upon time line, item six, comprised the handover of the military power of the republic to Yuan Shikai. This came about after Sun completed his residual duties as president on April 1. At that point, President Sun at last took his place as a private citizen of the Republic of China he had helped to found.

The Revolution in Hindsight

China's 1911 revolution was highly peculiar and, as historian James Sheridan phrases it, "curiously bland." Although Sun Yatsen's tireless promotion of the cause of revolution and leadership of the Revolutionary Alliance had fostered an atmosphere receptive to an overthrow of the Qing dynasty, he himself was not the driving force behind the event when it actually took place. Rather, the primary forces behind the overthrow of the dynasty were the provincial elites and the revolutionaries. Indeed, there is an irony even here: The provincial elites joined the revolution in large part to control the revolutionaries, who they feared might otherwise seek to threaten their privileges. The revolutionaries, in turn, were willing to compromise heavily with the elites because they viewed cooperation with them as their sole path to success. Overall, there was a wide range of opinion among the founders of the republic and anti-Manchuism was virtually the only point that everyone agreed on.

Whatever the 1911 revolution was, it was emphatically not a social revolution. The masses played no part in the revolution, and indeed, most peasants in the countryside were not even aware that it had taken place. Ordinary people continued to pay the same land rents to the same landlords as they had previously. Indeed, their land rents actually increased, as upper-level landlords moved to the cities and left rent collection in the hands of avaricious deputies unrestrained by any government. *Minsheng*—Sun Yatsen's third principle of people's livelihood—was sadly neglected as an objective during the revolution.

One aspect of the entire situation that must not be forgotten is the palpable anxiety that the revolutionaries felt vis-à-vis the privileged Western powers in China. If any part of the revolution displayed antiforeign overtones, the revolutionaries correctly reasoned, the Western powers would crush it immediately, just as they had crushed the Boxers. Accordingly, from the very beginning the proclamations of the revolutionaries featured emphatic reassurances that the new Chinese government would continue to observe China's various treaty obligations toward the West.

The revolutionaries' concerns—shared by Sun in Europe—were fully justified. Throughout October, 1911, the major Western powers maintained a dozen warships on high alert on the Yangzi River just outside of Wuhan. Moreover, these powers tightened their methods of collection on the substantial debt—stemming from treaties and loans—that China owed them. Specifically, they now arrogated to themselves the authority to control the collection, banking, and remittance of all customs revenue charged on goods brought into China. This circumstance alone demonstrates that the revolution in no way removed the basic power imbalance that China faced during the early twentieth century.

The revolution of 1911 nevertheless fits into a larger pattern in early twentieth-century history, namely, the decline of monarchies worldwide. At the beginning of the 1910s, most major countries continued to be governed by kings, emperors, and the like. However, developments associated with World War I would bring about the abolition of a great number of these monarchies, including those of Germany, Austria-Hungary, Russia, and the Ottoman Empire. In this respect, Sun Yatsen's insistence that his nation adopt a republican system of government turned out to be prescient on a global scale.

9

The Dream Goes Awry

Perhaps the saddest years in Sun Yatsen's life were the ones that directly followed his brief months as Provisional President of China in 1912. Essentially, the dream that Sun and other revolutionaries put forward was hijacked by military strongman Yuan Shikai. Yuan spent his four years as China's ruler attempting to solidify his control over the nation's political life. While Sun cooperated with Yuan at first—mainly to promote his own agenda of rapid modernization—he turned bitterly against Yuan once he had decided that his rule was gratuitously violent. From then on, Sun, with a modicum of Japanese support, opposed Yuan until his rule collapsed in 1916. Following Yuan's death in that year, the country degenerated into a state of warlordism that would continue in one form or another through the rest of Sun's life and even beyond.

With the anti-Qing revolution of 1911, the elites of China had abandoned two millennia of monarchies in favor of a republican government. The structure of this new government—the Republic of China—was established by the provisional constitution that the parliament passed while Sun was still president. Confusingly, this constitution created *two* heads of state: president and prime minister. The president was required to govern in accordance with the wishes of a cabinet comprised of ministers in charge of various government agencies. The prime minister, in turn, was the leading figure in this cabinet, tasked with promoting consensus within the cabinet and ensuring that the president's actions stayed within the limits of the law. President Yuan Shikai behaved at the beginning as though he accepted this system. In the absence of an elected parliament, he was able to choose the first prime minister, an ally who then appointed the other ministers of the cabinet. Within this cabinet, friends of Yuan garnered the most vital positions while Revolutionary Alliance members received less consequential posts.

Despite this display of favoritism, the new prime minister insisted that Yuan observe the mechanisms of republican government. When Yuan continued to act as he pleased, the prime minister and the four Revolutionary Alliance members in the cabinet all resigned in protest in June 1912. Ironically, this action played into Yuan's hands because Yuan simply appointed *closer* friends to the vacated positions. The cabinet was soon completely under his control.

An additional stipulation of the constitution called for elections to parliament to occur within six months of the passage of special laws to organize them, which placed the elections at the end of 1912 and beginning of 1913. While most Chinese did not receive the franchise, males over 21 with adequate education or tax payments did, rendering these elections far more broadly representative than the ones that were held for provincial assembly representatives back in 1909.

Adapting itself to its new context, the Revolutionary Alliance quickly reorganized itself as a parliamentary party. This party called itself the **Guomindang**, which means "Nationalist Party" (hereafter GMD). Conscious that rival parties had also appeared, the **GMD** absorbed a number of smaller parties to increase its size and the likelihood of victory. Sun Yatsen presided over the executive committee of the GMD, with Huang Xing as his cochair. However, the party primarily reflected the outlook of another prominent member, Song Jiaoren. Song was a perfect party man: He preferred collective leadership to individual power, trusted parliamentary institutions, and sought to win elections by cultivating powerful constituencies. Sun, in contrast, felt more comfortable operating through networks of personal relationships while maintaining an allegiance to socially progressive ideals. Song's main constituency—the provincial elites—showed little interest in the issue of people's livelihood, which displeased Sun. Indeed, Sun preferred to meet repeatedly with Yuan Shikai, who in the summer of 1912 never failed to treat Sun and his ideas with courtesy and respect.

Song nevertheless led the GMD to victory in the winter elections. Running on a conservative but strongly anti-Yuan platform, Song and the GMD managed to become the majority party in parliament. Having won, Song even began to discuss the possibility of impeaching Yuan for his earlier disregard of parliament. Despite Yuan's abuses of his position, it appeared as though a democratic system, complete with clashes and compromises, was steadily replacing China's age-old tradition of dynastic rule.

Sun and Railways

In the latter half of 1912, Sun Yatsen was not thinking very much about the political wrangling between Yuan Shikai and the GMD: He was preoccupied with railroads, railroads, and yet more railroads. Yuan appointed Sun as the republic's director of railways, a post he embraced with great gusto. From early September onward, Sun traveled continuously throughout central and south China, promoting his vision of a China crisscrossed by railroads to officials, journalists, and whoever else would listen.

Sun's interest in railroads was nothing new. Already in his 1894 letter to Li Hongzhang he had stated that "in all countries that have railroads, goods can be shipped unhindered to any corner, while in those without railroads, the circulation of goods is hampered at every turn, as in a state of paralysis." Although a number of railroads had been built in China in the intervening years, they were concentrated in resource-rich Manchuria, leaving the rest of the country nearly untouched. This distressed Sun, who flatly proclaimed in 1912 that "the wealth of a nation can be judged by the mileage of [its] railroads."

Sun's fixation on railroads becomes more understandable when we consider that they comprised the largest industrial enterprise in early twentieth-century China, transporting tens of millions of passengers and thousands of tons of cargo annually. Sun also lived in an era when, internationally, there was a widespread belief that railroads were the best way to generate economic growth in a country. Certainly they had helped unite such geographically large countries as the United States, Canada, and Russia, whose wide-flung parts otherwise had little communication with each other. With their potential to foster national strength, freedom of movement, *and* widespread economic uplift, railroads appeared to partake of all three of Sun's People's Principles, namely, nationalism, democracy, and people's livelihood.

Sun quickly began to create grandiose plans for a comprehensive rail system for China. At first, he mistakenly believed that China was five times as large as the United States, so he asserted that China's rail system would have to be five times as large as well! Even after correcting this error, he still held that China should build 70,000 miles of railroads (it had well under 10,000 miles at the time) and that it could do so within 10 years. That many people regarded this as unrealistic only increased his obstinacy on the issue.

The core of Sun's plan was to have two trunk lines built horizontally across China. These lines would run northeast to northwest and southeast to southwest, respectively. In more detailed plans that he later set out in *The International Development of China* (1919), Sun explained that his intent was to link coastal urban centers to such resource-rich peripheries as Xinjiang province (northwestern China), with its meat and wool, and Tibet (southwestern China), with its minerals, coal, and natural gas. Railroads that reached those peripheries could then link the Chinese market to outside rail systems that led to India, the Middle East, and beyond. In short, politics and economics would intertwine: Railroads to distant regions of China would both unite the country and yield quick profits for canny investors.

The actual conditions for railroad construction in China in the 1910s were a far cry from what Sun envisioned. First of all, even under Yuan Shikai China lacked the sort of strong central government that could undertake the scale of rail construction that Sun recommended. China had quietly divided into regions, each of which sought to govern its own affairs rather than contribute its resources to any long-term national undertaking. Without a commitment to railroads from either the center—Yuan was only mildly interested—or the provinces, massive railroad construction was unlikely.

A still greater difficulty was that China's international context was inhospitable to Sun's plans. If China was not the "hypo-colony" that Sun claimed, it was nevertheless a semicolony. This had implications for railroads. It meant, first, that China possessed multiple rail systems run by an array of foreign countries. Each major line operated its own mechanical shops and supply depots, with lines diverging even on which track gauge to use. In this respect, railroads were acting as a *dis*integrating force in China. Moreover, China was dependent on foreign lenders for seed capital and these lenders were becoming less generous: Following the 1911 revolution, Western banking consortia offered their railroad loans for shorter terms at higher rates of interest. Under these circumstances, a railroad would have to show high profits simply to break even. Finally, China was not able to protect its fledgling industries with substantial import tariffs the way truly sovereign countries could. This made it very difficult for Chinese companies to produce, for example, iron rail that could compete with the cost of identical rail imported from abroad. As a result, even the new railroads that *were* built would not necessarily stimulate China's economy. All in all, a mix of domestic and foreign circumstances seemed to conspire to prevent Sun's rail dreams from ever coming true.

Despite the insuperable obstacles of the time, Sun's grand vision of a transportation infrastructure that could bind together China's disparate regions has enjoyed a respectable afterlife. Sun insisted that wherever there were roads in China, there could also be railroads. Indeed, on a detailed map that Sun had drawn of his plans, he placed railroads even across the icy highlands of Tibet in present-day China's southwest. This seemed incredible to Sun's interlocutors at the time, yet in the year 2006, the Chinese government successfully completed a major railway that links China's northeast to its southwest and crosses those same highlands. Actually, in the twenty-first century, it is not so much China's rail system as its rapidly expanding highway system that is steadily realizing Sun's dream of easy, rapid movement throughout China. Interestingly, Sun anticipated this as well, emphasizing in his *The International Development of China* the importance of automobiles to China's future. All in all, Sun's vision of a comprehensive rail system addressed his country's future challenges much better than it did the exigencies of his day. And it reflected once again his eager search for a shortcut to strengthen China in the modern world.

Yuan Shikai Becomes a Dictator

By an unhappy coincidence, the next major event in China's history after the parliamentary elections of 1912–1913 took place at Shanghai's main rail station. On March 20, 1913, 31-year-old Song Jiaoren was standing on the platform at the station, ready to board a train that would take him to his new post as the chief representative of the GMD in Beijing. At that moment, a gunman shot and killed him. The gunman and others associated with him later died under mysterious circumstances, but it appears evident that Yuan Shikai was behind the murder.

With the assassination of Song Jiaoren, the cause of representative government in China suffered a severe setback. As historian John King Fairbank has stated, this assassination "demonstrated a principle (that the ruler is above the law) and a tactic (that opponents can best be checked by eliminating their leader) which have strangled democracy in China ever since." What took shape next between Yuan and his opponents was an unequal struggle in which Yuan postured as China's wise protector, while his opponents scrambled to expose his many injustices. The British greatly assisted Yuan's side of this struggle. Less than a month after Song's assassination, a five-nation banking consortium led by Great Britain provided Yuan's government with a huge "Reorganization Loan" worth 25 million British pounds. This loan effectually propped up Yuan's government, which was starving for other sources of funds. Conversely, it also rendered that government more dependent on British and other foreigners who viewed it as the protector of their interests.

Sun Yatsen utterly opposed Yuan Shikai from the moment he learned of Song's assassination onward. This contrasted with the responses of many other GMD revolutionaries, who sought to let the legal system determine who lay behind the crime. Sun, however, had reentered the frame of mind that he had possessed while attacking the Qing dynasty: The current government, he again believed, formed an absolute obstacle to China's advancement as a modern nation. Accordingly, in mid-1913, he called for a **"Second Revolution"** in the spirit of the revolution of 1911 to overthrow Yuan Shikai.

While Sun was undoubtedly sincere in his disgust at Yuan's autocratic methods, another crucial factor was involved. When the assassination of Song took place, Sun was visiting Japan, where he had received a royal welcome from Japan's political and industrial elites. Since the 1911 revolution, Japan had become the second largest foreign investor in China after Great Britain. Yuan's overall policy was to court British favor while displaying hostility to Japan, a country he deeply feared. Japanese circles, in turn, looked for a potential counterweight to Yuan and found— Sun Yatsen. Sun had prestige as a senior revolutionary and a former president of the Chinese republic. He was also friendly to Japan and seemed unlikely to shut Japan out of China as Yuan was seeking to do. Accordingly, Japanese officials encouraged Sun's plans for a Second Revolution.

After Yuan Shikai dismissed pro-GMD military governors in central Chinese provinces in July 1913, GMD leaders, too, began to seek a military showdown with Yuan's forces. The primary showdown took place during two weeks in mid-July in the vicinity of Nanjing. Similarly to 1911, several provinces announced their secession from the central government. This time, however, revolutionary forces were on the defensive from the start, with inadequate arms and poor organization. Huang Xing led the forces that fought Yuan but withdrew them from a battle over Nanjing once it became clear that victory would be impossible. While some fighting continued into August in other areas, Yuan's army completely suppressed the attempt at revolution by early September.

Sun's Second Revolution—more a series of skirmishes—could not succeed because none of the conditions for victory were present. In contrast to the pervasive antigovernment sentiment of 1911, most of China's provincial elites in 1913 favored Yuan, regarding him as a tough man for tough times. Moreover, foreign governments did not remain neutral—as we have seen, they viewed Yuan as the guarantor of their interests. Finally, many GMD members themselves hesitated to wage a prolonged war against Yuan because they felt that such a war would only weaken China as a whole.

After the Second Revolution collapsed, Sun returned to Japan, though without the fanfare of his previous visit. While still in Tokyo, Sun created a new organization in July 1913 called the Chinese Revolutionary Party. It was to be a small, tight organization that would be strictly bound by loyalty to him. In every respect, it would contrast with the much looser and more open organization of the GMD, which Sun now viewed as a failure. Sun had members of the new organization swear an oath of personal allegiance to him. He also told them, "I dare say that, but for me, there are no guides to the revolution. . . . There are many things you do not understand. . . . You should blindly follow me." Many GMD revolutionaries, including Huang Xing, refused to swear allegiance. Undeterred, Sun gradually turned to the Shanghai business underworld for new followers to replace those who had turned away.

While Sun regrouped in Tokyo, Yuan employed increasingly brazen methods to consolidate his control over the Chinese government. Thus, over the course of the next year and a half, he would concoct reasons to disband the GMD (November 1913), dissolve the elected parliament (January 1914), and promulgate a new constitution that would permit him to rule indefinitely (May 1914). While all of this was happening, Yuan also imposed martial law, closed numerous newspapers, and used secret police to execute thousands of people. Yuan Shikai and his henchmen were riding high and by mid-1914, he had amassed as much power for himself as the emperors of the Qing dynasty had possessed.

Sun's Opportunism, Yuan's Fall

One of the most catastrophic events of the twentieth century, World War I, began in Western Europe less than three months after Yuan promulgated the constitution that swelled his power. While the war was based around intra-European struggles in which China had little stake, side-effects of the war would help shape the Chinese context in which Sun operated for the remainder of the 1910s.

Both belligerent parties to the war—the Allied Powers and the Central Powers—were represented among the nations that possessed spheres of influence in China. Among the Central Powers, Germany possessed a sphere of influence in Shandong province, near Beijing. The Japanese government quickly joined the Allied side in the war, following which its army attacked and defeated German forces in Shandong. Several months after this had taken place, in January 1915, Japanese Prime Minister Ōkuma Shigenobu presented the Chinese government of Yuan Shikai with a list of Twenty-One Demands. If Yuan acceded to the demands, Japanese would receive a wide range of privileges in China such as special economic rights in regions in which the Japanese government had an especially strong interest. Essentially, the Japanese government was seeking the preeminent position among foreign powers in China. Indeed, the last category of demands within the list went further and would have made China into virtually a protectorate of Japan. Yuan Shikai attempted to excite Western outrage against Japan by publicizing its demands, but was able to attract little attention against the backdrop of World War I. In the end, he gave in to all of the demands except those in the last category, leading many previously supportive Chinese to conclude that their president had betrayed his country.

Sun's response to the entire situation is revealing. In public, he criticized Yuan as many other Chinese had done. Privately, however, he attempted to offer the Japanese government even more extensive privileges than it had demanded from Yuan! These included promises to implement Japanese instructions for reforming China's government and military, allow Japanese commercial domination of China through preferential banking arrangements, and so on. Such promises were contingent, of course, on Sun being able to resume a position of rulership in China—something that he could only have achieved with colossal infusions of Japanese military aid. Nevertheless, the extent of his eagerness to please is painfully clear in a secret letter to Prime Minister Ōkuma in which he describes China as a potential India—that is, a resource-rich colony—that would be available to Japan if only it armed and assisted anti-Yuan forces. Sentiments such as these place Sun in a category by himself among Chinese nationalists, virtually all of whom were by now intensely hostile to Japanese ambitions in China.

As the commotion over the Twenty-One Demands continued, Yuan prepared for a bizarre new venture: having himself installed as the emperor of a new Chinese dynasty! To achieve this new ambition, Yuan orchestrated a popular movement, replete with petitions and demonstrations, that demanded his coronation. On December 12, 1915, he made a show of yielding to the movement and declared that his reign as emperor would begin on January 1, 1916.

Yuan's fantasy was quickly smashed. As in 1911 and 1913, once again provinces began to declare their independence from the central government. This time the first to secede was the remote province of Yunnan, whose military leader quickly created a "National Protection Army" to oppose Yuan's plans. As other southern provinces steadily seceded, Yuan first delayed and then, in March 1916, cancelled his coronation.

There were good reasons for the vehement backlash against Yuan's plans. The prestige of monarchy in China had been decimated by the 1911 revolution. Moreover, Yuan's own military governors and longtime followers regarded his coronation plan as an attempt to consolidate his control at their expense. Oddly enough, Sun Yatsen played only a negligible role in the new anti-Yuan movement. He did attempt to rally the Chinese navy to attack targets in Shanghai in December 1915, but the attack was badly botched and brought only embarrassment. Instead, it was the jilted military governors who took center stage.

Yuan, a leader who had always exuded power and control, now backpedaled furiously to conciliate his many critics. Provinces continued to secede no matter what he did and even a leading Beiyang Army general recommended that he resign. Evidently embittered by the trend of events, Yuan Shikai suddenly died of uremia in June 1916.

Sun revealed a great deal regarding his political agenda and style through his responses to Yuan in the early 1910s. When Sun became Provisional President in 1912, he had sought to placate Yuan, whom he offered the presidency. Indeed, even after Yuan became president and began to display authoritarian tendencies, Sun continued to cultivate his friendship and accepted the directorship of railways from him. The turning point came with the assassination of Song Jiaoren. This event prompted Sun to launch his Second Revolution in hopes of overthrowing Yuan. Later, when Yuan tried to have himself crowned as emperor, Sun maintained his resistance to him, although by this time others had taken the lead. The overall pattern among Sun's various responses is that he appreciated Yuan as a paternalistic statesman—preferring his company to that of members of his own GMD—but utterly rejected him as a dictator or emperor. Sun's approach, in practice, was to promote the centralization of power—whether that of Yuan or that of himself—while vehemently opposing those who abused that power once it was centrally collected.

The Turn to Warlordism

Almost immediately after Yuan Shikai died, China split into regions ruled by rapacious warlords. This new phenomenon—warlordism—forms the continuous backdrop for the remainder of Sun Yatsen's career. Sun in the past had typically faced a single overwhelming enemy: the Qing dynasty until 1911 and Yuan Shikai's dictatorship from 1913 until 1916. In contrast, during the final decade of his life, the political scene was far more complex and required an incredible degree of dexterity from all participants. Sun would make numerous mistakes, trusting some people whom he ought to have viewed suspiciously and denouncing others with whom he should have cooperated. Nevertheless, his perseverance under adversity was striking. As Sun biographer Harold Schiffrin has stated, "More gifted contemporaries made their bids for power, failed, and fell by the wayside, but Sun always came back from defeat, ready to adjust to a new situation."

At first glance, there was a certain familiarity to the circumstances that followed Yuan Shikai's death. Li Yuanhong, a national figure since his role in the 1911 revolution, immediately succeeded Yuan as president. As part of his effort to restore normalcy, Li reconvened the parliament that had been elected in 1912–1913 and reinstated the provisional constitution of 1912. Nevertheless, the reconvened parliament proved to be exceptionally open to bribery, with the result that it hemorrhaged credibility. Moreover, the real show in Chinese politics increasingly lay outside Beijing, in the rural areas where armies large and small were being mustered.

Warlordism is something that often appears in countries whose central governments have more or less collapsed. Much like feudalism, it is an attempt to create a degree of local order through personal relationships in an environment in which national order has disappeared. In contrast to the feudal systems of medieval Europe and Japan, however, warlordism is highly unstable. The bonds of loyalty among military participants are weak, yielding a spectacle of prolonged conflict among ever-shifting groups. As a result, warlordism presents a nearly intractable problem for anyone—such as Sun Yatsen—who might seek to end it: Any new military force that is deployed to achieve national unification runs the continual risk of instead becoming one more party to the conflict.

The ultimate origins of China's new warlordism trace back to the regionally based armies that the Qing dynasty had sanctioned a half century earlier to suppress the Taiping Rebellion. The more immediate roots, however, lay with Yuan Shikai, who had appointed 10 of his Beiyang Army generals as provincial military governors. Soon after Yuan's death, these generals became the first generation of warlords. Their sway lasted only a few years, however, and after 1920, new figures established themselves as the primary warlords of the land.

Both Yuan's generals and the later warlords espoused a wide range of ideologies and in fact a number of them actually made efforts at social reform. Nevertheless, they were invariably cruel when their power was threatened—which under the circumstances was a very frequent occurrence. Still worse for ordinary Chinese, they were continually short of money to pay their troops, leading them to impose a bewildering variety of taxes on every conceivable product and activity. Notwithstanding their self-image as swashbuckling heroes, the warlords brought misery into most of the lives they touched.

It is worth underscoring that Sun Yatsen lived out the final decade of his life against the frightening backdrop of warlord domination. Sun's overall response to this new challenge would be to condemn warlordism, negotiate with some of the warlords, and, once all else had failed, ally his party with the Soviet Union to develop a force more powerful than any warlord coalition. The bases of his operations would be Guangzhou and Shanghai, two of China's largest and most innovative cities. Indeed, it was in Shanghai that dramatic changes overturned his family life, to which we now turn.

CHAPTER

10

Interlude: Sun's Marriages

One of the most carefully researched biographies of Sun Yatsen in English is Columbia professor C. Martin Wilbur's *Sun Yat-sen: Frustrated Patriot.* This biography, almost 300 pages in length, contains one section just four pages long titled "The Private Man." In that section, Wilbur rapidly surveys Sun's friends, his marriages, his children, and several of his personal habits. What did he conclude regarding the private Sun? "'Dead serious' are suitable words for his entire life . . ." Throughout his adult career, Sun dedicated his energies to the creation of a modern, powerful, republican China, and this appears to have left little room for anything else.

Sun's overwhelming earnestness notwithstanding, his family affairs, and especially his marriages, remain important. Indeed, Sun's behavior in his three marriages neatly expresses the protean character that he shared with his times. His first marriage displayed his traditionality, as he traveled the world for his work while leaving his wife behind to take care of his children and parents. His second marriage displayed his abiding connection to Japan, as he wedded a young Japanese woman whom he met during his residence in that country. Finally, his third marriage displayed his modernity, as he and his wife entered a partnership that transformed his work into a joint endeavor.

Sun's family relationships are important in still another way. His final wife, **Soong Qingling**, outlived him by more than 50 years and became a powerful politician and role model in her own right. Her sisters and brothers, in turn, were tremendously influential in early twentieth-century China and her future brother-in-law, **Chiang Kaishek**, went on to rule the country for more than 20 years. Accordingly, when Chinese people today read or hear about the Soong family and Chiang Kaishek, respectively, they also think of Sun. Sun's marriage to a member of the Soong family draws him into their story, while a Soong family member's marriage to him draws them into *his* story. Family ties are extremely important in Chinese life and Sun's own ties have given his name, image, and ideas even greater exposure than they already possessed.

Finally, it must be acknowledged that despite his vaunted earnestness, Sun was something of a philanderer. This emerges in an amusing episode that occurred while he was in Japan. Once, during a conversation between Sun and his friend

Inukai Tsuyoshi, Inukai asked Sun what his favorite thing was. Sun predictably answered, "Revolution." Inukai responded that everyone knew that that was the case, so what was his next favorite thing? Sun noticed Inukai's wife nearby and did not answer. When Inukai pressed him for a response, he answered, "Woman." As we will see, Sun's behavior during his adult life suggests that he was speaking the unvarnished truth.

A note of warning before we begin: This chapter is truly an interlude, albeit a vital one. It ranges widely through time, covering events as disparate as Sun's marriage to his first wife in the 1880s and the death of his final wife a full century later. While the bulk of the chapter focuses on the period of Sun's revolutionary career, his family members carried his legacy forward through their own activities long after his career ended. To understand these dynamics, we will at times venture into a future that Sun inhabited as a symbol rather than as the enterprising, conflicted human being whose activities we have been following.

Sun's Relationships Before the Revolution

Sun Yatsen married his first wife, Lu Muzhen, in 1884, when he was 17 years old. Lu was only 16 then, the daughter of a local merchant family. Her marriage with Sun was completely arranged between her relatives and Sun's—a traditional Chinese marriage, created with the primary objective of linking two families together. Upon marrying, Lu stayed with Sun's family and took care of his parents while he pursued his medical training in Guangzhou and Hong Kong. After Sun's father died in 1888, Lu continued to look after Sun's elderly mother in his native village of Cuiheng until his first Guangzhou Uprising fizzled in 1895. At that point, all of Sun's relatives had to leave China rapidly to escape the wrath of the Qing government.

As of 1895, Sun's family was small, comprising his mother, his wife, and his son **Sun Fo**, who was just four years old. Together they escaped the country and moved to Honolulu, where they lived with Sun's wealthy brother Sun Mei. In 1896, Lu gave birth successively to two daughters. The family remained in Hawaii for more than a decade, returning to China only in 1907. Upon his return, Sun Mei lived first in Hong Kong and then in Macao, which eventually became Lu's permanent home. Throughout all of this, Lu concentrated on fulfilling the primary traditional female role of attending to household affairs. Embracing that role, she did not—to our knowledge—criticize Sun for his lengthy absences from home.

Inasmuch as Sun's children had received their early education in Hawaii, it is understandable that they later attended schools in the United States. Sun Fo, for example, entered the University of California at Berkeley in 1911. Returning to China for his father's term as Provisional President, he afterward left again for California, this time with his sisters in tow. Tragically, the elder of the sisters died of a fatal illness in 1913. Her untimely death in that year brought great distress to her father, who was at the same time waging his abortive Second Revolution against Yuan Shikai. Sun Fo, meanwhile, remained in school and eventually completed a master's degree at Columbia University. Upon returning to China in 1917, he embarked on a lengthy and distinguished career of service to the governments that his father Sun Yatsen, and later Sun's successor Chiang Kaishek, created.

In her later years, Lu Muzhen lived in a large house in Macao that Sun Fo had given her—a house adorned with portraits of Sun Yatsen. Although Sun quietly divorced Lu in 1915, the two remained in friendly contact and Sun paid her alimony money. Focused on performing charitable services for the poor and sick, she far outlived her ex-husband Sun, dying in Macao in 1952.

Sun had other early relationships besides that with Lu Muzhen. Around 1890, while Sun was still studying medicine, one of his three "Great Bandit" friends, Chen Shaobai, introduced him to a woman from Hong Kong named Chen Cuifen. Sun entered a relationship with Chen and she accompanied him when he escaped to Hawaii after the Guangzhou Uprising of 1895. Thereafter, for at least 15 years, she traveled alongside Sun and performed housework for him while he undertook his revolutionary activities. There was evidently no jealousy between Lu and Chen because Chen was playing the traditional role of concubine and Lu accepted that. Indeed, the Sun family as a whole took her under their wing, with Lu in particular regarding Chen as effectually a sister. Like most of the women with whom Sun maintained relationships, Chen far outlived him while refusing to remarry.

Sun Yatsen had one other romantic relationship prior to the 1911 revolution, although this one remained a family secret for decades after his death. The relationship, a common-law marriage with a Japanese woman, was uncovered by Kubota Bunji, a Japanese researcher on Sun. When Sun was living undercover in Yokohama's Chinatown in 1898, he hid for a time with the family of a Mr. Ōtsuki, a Japanese merchant engaged in trade with Chinese firms. Mr. Ōtsuki had a daughter, Kaori, whom Sun found very attractive. When Sun returned to Japan in 1901, he sought to marry Kaori despite their wide disparity in ages: He was 36, while she was 14! While this was acceptable to Chinese custom at the time, it was highly unusual in Japan. Consequently, when Sun asked the girl's grandfather for permission to marry her, he angrily turned him down. Still eager to marry Kaori, Sun proposed to her directly the next year and she accepted. They held a simple wedding ceremony in Yokohama, following which Sun returned to his fundraising overseas. He returned to Yokohama to see his wife in 1905 and in 1906 she gave birth to a daughter. Even so, he left Japan again before the daughter was born. He never saw either the mother or the daughter subsequently, although he maintained contact with Kaori by mail.

Kaori later remarried twice. Soon after Sun's daughter was born, Kaori adopted her out to another family, with the result that the daughter's name—Miyakawa Fumiko—does not include either the Sun or the Ōtsuki family name. In the 1980s, when the relationship with Sun first came to light, a Japanese reporter visited the elderly Miyakawa and asked her about it. She stated, "I learned that I'm Sun Yatsen's daughter from my mother, but I considered Sun's family situation and never made it public." Evidently, Sun's relatives in the United

States had long been aware that he had had a Japanese wife and daughter but did not know anything further about the relationship.

Sun and Soong Qingling

Sun Yatsen met his third and final wife, Soong Qingling, through contacts he had much earlier established among Chinese Christians in Shanghai. His primary link with these Christians came through a single, striking figure with the adopted name Charles Jones Soong. Like Sun himself, Charles—invariably called Charlie—came from the far south of China. Also like Sun, **Charlie Soong** spent most of his teenage years in an English-language environment, specifically, the American South. Although Charlie returned to China in his twenties to serve as a missionary, he quickly discovered that he was even more suited for work as a comprador, that is, a business intermediary between Western and Chinese merchants.

Charlie married a devout Chinese Christian in 1887 and they rapidly began to have children—six in all. Three of these were daughters, the famous "Soong sisters" who became so well known for their marriages and strong personalities. In order of birth, the daughters were Ailing (b. 1888), Qingling (b. 1892), and Meiling (b. 1897). In a day when Chinese girls typically received little education, Charlie's daughters attended the leading missionary school in Shanghai, the McTyeire School for Girls.

Sun first became acquainted with Charlie at a Shanghai Methodist church, where they met after services. It was 1894, and Sun was on his way north to visit Li Hongzhang and present him with his famous letter. Sun and Charlie had a great deal in common, including not only Christianity and a shared dialect but secret society contacts, foreign education, and a parvenu status within Chinese society. The two figures forged a firm friendship and in the coming years, Sun would stay regularly at Charlie's home and become a familiar figure to his children.

When the Soong sisters came of age, they attended Wesleyan College in Macon, Georgia, thereby becoming the first Chinese women to receive higher education in the United States. Indeed, middle-daughter Qingling was still attending Wesleyan in 1911 when the Chinese Revolution broke out. According to her classmates there, Qingling responded to news of the revolution by climbing up on a chair in her dormitory room, tearing down the imperial Chinese flag on the wall, hanging up the new five-colored flag, and yelling out, "Down with the dragon! Up with the flag of the republic!" To underscore her excitement, she also wrote an article on the subject for Wesleyan's literary magazine with the triumphant title "The Greatest Event of the Twentieth Century."

Back in China, Charlie was in frequent contact with Sun during 1912. Indeed, after Sun became Director of Railways he appointed Charlie as his treasurer and hired Soong Ailing, with her excellent English skills, as his secretary. As Sun and Ailing worked together, the two gradually fell in love. In 1913, Sun asked Charlie for permission to marry Ailing but he refused. Soon afterward, Ailing began a romance with H. H. Kung, an especially wealthy young man with American connections. After they married, Kung utilized his positions in banking and later in government to become one of the richest people on earth.

Following the failure of the Second Revolution in mid-1913, Sun and the entire Soong family escaped to Japan where they were able to operate beyond the reach of Yuan Shikai's agents. Qingling, already an avid admirer of Sun, traveled to Japan to join her family as soon as she graduated from Wesleyan. She visited Sun a number of times with her father and, beginning in 1914, replaced Ailing as Sun's secretary. A new romance soon bloomed. Before long Sun and Qingling decided to marry, although they attempted to keep their relationship hidden from Qingling's parents as long as possible. At the time, Sun was 49 years of age while Qingling was just 22.

Long after Sun's death in 1925, Qingling described her feelings toward Sun during this period as follows: "It was a romantic girl's idea when I ran away to work for him—but a good one. I wanted to help save China and Dr. Sun was the one man who could do it. So I wanted to help him." This was far from the outlook of Qingling's parents, who had already publicly announced her engagement to a promising young man. When Qingling insisted that she would not go through with the marriage because of her prior commitment to Sun, her parents were furious. Charlie was especially upset, even heartbroken, because he viewed himself as having been betrayed by both his best friend and his daughter.

Religiously speaking, the greatest difficulty was that Sun was still married to Lu Muzhen. From the Christian standpoint of Qingling's parents, Sun could not remarry unless he first divorced Lu. In a Chinese context, however, divorce would have signaled that Lu had failed in her duties as a Chinese wife, which everyone knew to be untrue. Sun's solution was to divorce Lu secretly in Japan so as to spare her any embarrassment in China. While this approach satisfied Lu, it did not fully appease Qingling's parents, as we shall see presently.

In 1915, the Soong family was back in Shanghai even as Sun remained in Japan. Physical distance alone made the relationship between Sun and Qingling difficult to sustain. Moreover, Charlie tried to confine Qingling to her upstairs bedroom. Qingling, however, was audacious. First, she wrote Sun a letter that her maid smuggled out for her. After she received Sun's response, she appealed once more to her father, who now *locked* her in the bedroom. This time she arranged with her maid to climb out the window, using a ladder that the maid held. Upon escaping, she immediately went to the Shanghai dockyard and sailed for Japan. She and Sun married in Tokyo on October 25, 1915, the day after she arrived.

The marriage between Sun and Qingling contrasted sharply with that between Sun and Lu. It was a modern-style romantic marriage to which both partners remained loyal. In 1917, when Sun established a new revolutionary government in Guangzhou, Qingling made her first public appearances as "Madame Sun." In a country where women traditionally stayed at home rather than taking part in their husbands' social lives, the spectacle of this young, stylish, and articulate woman at her husband's side drew fascinated attention. As she attended Sun's many political speeches, she was invariably the only woman present. Indeed, her behavior was daring even in a global context: As of the early twentieth century, politicians' wives the world over typically refrained from participating in the workaday aspects of their husbands' careers.

Sun welcomed Qingling's attendance at the speeches: After all, she not only continued to serve as his secretary but now functioned as a crucial political advisor. Qingling, in turn, sought to be a part of every aspect of her husband's life. Even with all of her enthusiasm, however, she could find it nerve-wracking to be in the audience as he lectured: "He made it all up on the spur of the moment. It all depended on the political situation and the audience. I would be nervous as a cat, sitting next to him on the platform and wondering what was coming next." Her self-description here applies with equal strength to her career after Sun's death, when she became a prominent political figure despite her intense and persistent shyness.

To follow Qingling into her later life requires that we delve into the final decade of Sun's life and beyond. As we do so, we shall observe how Sun's ideas and especially his prestige as a symbol of Chinese nationalism carried into bewilderingly new contexts in the middle twentieth century and beyond.

Under the changed global circumstances of the early 1920s, Sun Yatsen decided to ally the GMD with the Soviet Union, despite his disagreement with aspects of that country's Communist ideology. Given his Guangzhou government's desperate need for aid, he felt that he had little choice. The alliance was effectually a coalition between the GMD and the **Chinese Communist Party** (hereafter CCP), which the Soviet Union was sponsoring at the time. Although the alliance was controversial within his party, it did provide Sun with funds to set up a military academy and train a large army. Sun appointed Chiang Kaishek, a figure whom he had originally met through contacts in the Shanghai underworld, to lead the military academy. Qingling, meanwhile, strongly backed Sun's decision to enter the alliance, displaying the first signs of a pro-Soviet orientation that she would maintain for the rest of her life.

By the time Sun Yatsen died in early 1925, he had become one of China's most popular politicians. Subsequently, an array of political figures would attempt to claim his legacy in one form or another. One of these figures was Chiang Kaishek, who proposed marriage to Qingling shortly after her husband's death. Qingling quickly rejected the proposal, which she viewed as a crude political maneuver to appropriate Sun's prestige. From this time onward, she was highly suspicious of Chiang, who soon became the leading figure in the rapidly growing GMD.

Chiang temporarily maintained Sun's alliance with the Soviet Union, employing Soviet assistance to launch a massive military campaign to reunite China. As his armies conquered the warlords of south and central China in 1926–1927, a sharp internal split developed between the right wing of the GMD, which wanted to end the alliance with the Soviets, and the left wing of the GMD, which sought to keep the alliance intact. The "GMD Right" was concentrated in Nanjing, where Chiang had established his military headquarters, while the "GMD Left" installed itself in Wuhan. As her role in the Wuhan regime expanded, Qingling steadily became the most widely known female revolutionary in the world, dubbed "China's Joan of Arc" by some American journalists.

When Chiang's forces took over Shanghai, they massacred thousands of Communist workers with whom the GMD was still formally allied. This action created a definitive rupture with the Soviet Union while also deepening the right/left split within the GMD. Following his attack on Communist forces, Chiang exerted intense political and military pressure on the GMD Left in Wuhan. As part of this effort, he sent members of the Soong family to persuade Qingling to accede to his leadership. She refused.

Indeed, on July 14, 1927, as Wuhan was increasingly overrun by Chiang's agents, she went beyond refusal. On that day, she released a "Statement in Protest Against the Violation of Sun Yatsen's Revolutionary Principles and Policies," a blistering attack on Chiang's leadership of the GMD. The statement was the most important political declaration of her life. Continuously invoking Sun, the statement argued that the GMD under Chiang had betrayed the Chinese Revolution, which was supposed to be a revolution in people's livelihood, that is, in the living conditions of China's toiling masses. With this declaration, Qingling burned most of her bridges to her quintessentially well-connected family. Lacking their protection for anything beyond her bare personal safety, she escaped China after Chiang triumphed over the Wuhan government, taking refuge in Moscow.

While Qingling was busy recasting Sun Yatsen's legacy in a radical direction, Chiang was busy recasting his legacy in an emphatically conservative one. Chiang was also courting Qingling's sister Meiling! Their romance led directly to wedding preparations, which were announced by the end of the summer of 1927. Qingling, in Moscow, declared that she would rather die than see her sister marry Chiang. Nevertheless, Meiling firmly believed (as Chiang himself did) that Chiang was destined to save China from its chaotic circumstances. In that respect, her reason for marrying Chiang closely resembled Qingling's reason for marrying Sun. With idealism triumphing once more in the Soong family, Chiang became the brother-in-law of the late Sun Yatsen.

Meanwhile, Qingling—now the black sheep of her family—became intensely active in the international left in Europe and elsewhere. Within this context, she cultivated a markedly feminist voice, arguing passionately that radical revolutions needed to empower women as well as the male working class. Overall, her views broadly conformed to those of the global left—including even a positive appraisal of Soviet dictator Joseph Stalin—without surrendering the distinctiveness of her personal perspective. This perspective carried the weight that it did largely because of her youthful marriage to Sun Yatsen.

In 1937, the militarist government of Japan launched a full-scale invasion of the Republic of China, which continued to be led by Chiang Kaishek. The invasion scored quick successes, capturing most of China's major cities within a year. Under the desperate circumstances, the GMD and the CCP formed a second, temporary alliance to drive out the Japanese invaders. This political rapprochement led to a personal rapprochement among the Soong sisters, who appeared several times in public together in 1940 to promote the united war effort against Japan. Following the Allied victory over Japan in 1945, they quickly returned to opposite sides of the political fence.

During the late 1940s, Qingling lent the prestige of her connection to Sun Yatsen to the CCP's rise to power. The Communist Party was led by **Mao Zedong,** whom Qingling said she distrusted less than other political figures. When the party proved victorious in a civil war with Chiang Kaishek's GMD, Mao announced the creation of a new government, the People's Republic of China (hereafter PRC), on October 1, 1949. Mao made the dramatic announcement from the viewing stand at Tiananmen Square in Beijing with Qingling standing near him as a leading supporter.

After 1949, Qingling held a variety of ceremonial positions in China's new Communist government. She tried to join the Communist party but the party told her that her voice carried more weight if she did not become a member. Meanwhile, she kept herself occupied in other ways, editing a **PRC** magazine in English and directing a charitable organization for impoverished children. She also enjoyed two residences: a Western-style house in Shanghai that her father built and a palatial residence in Beijing where the last emperor of the Qing dynasty was born. When Qingling made public speeches, she invariably stressed the relevance of Sun Yatsen's Three People's Principles to the new challenges that China faced.

In all, Soong Qingling played the role of Sun Yatsen's widow for a full 56 years. Only a few weeks before her death from leukemia in Beijing in 1981, the CCP finally inducted her as a member. When an American journalist asked Qingling what the greatest accomplishment of her life had been, she answered, "The fact that I was loyal to Dr. Sun from the day I met him until his death."

11

The South Secedes

In the late 1910s and early 1920s, the ultimate goal of both Sun Yatsen and the warlords was to acquire control over Beijing. Throughout most of the warlord era, the city retained the skeletal frame of the republican system that Sun and others had established in 1912, namely, the offices of president and prime minister and the institutions of cabinet and parliament. Staffing these offices and institutions with their own handpicked representatives, rival coalitions of warlords rapidly replaced each other. Why was Beijing so important? The answer is simple: The Western powers provided support to whoever managed to dominate the city. They did this because they collected customs dues at China's borders—using the dues to help pay off its massive debts—and they undertook this task in the name of the Beijing government. An operating "Beijing government" thus needed to exist, even if in reality it ruled over only a small area of the country.

World War I, China, and Sun

When Yuan Shikai died suddenly in mid-1916, Li Yuanhong became the next president and Duan Qirui, one of Yuan's senior commanders, became the prime minister. Duan behaved like a smaller-scale version of Yuan: Over time, he abolished the provisional constitution, reduced the size of the electorate, and created a new parliament more to his liking. He also did something else, something that brought Sun Yatsen back into the political spotlight after four years of relative obscurity. Without seeking approval from either the cabinet or the parliament, on May 14, 1917, Duan Qirui declared war on Germany, thereby placing China on the side of the Allied powers in World War I.

Although World War I raged primarily in Europe, the two alliances that fought there fiercely competed for the support and resources of countries around the world. Year 1917 marked a period of considerable shakeups for the Allied powers in this regard: Russia withdrew from the Allied side, while the United States joined it in response to German attacks. As the United States entered the war, it placed diplomatic pressure on nations such as China to join the struggle against Germany and its allies.

Duan welcomed the suggestion of the U.S. government. Earlier in the war, Japan, already an Allied power, had taken over much of Shandong province, where Germany maintained a sphere of influence. Duan expected that the Allied side would win the war and that when it did, it would reward China for its assistance by compelling Japan to return Shandong to China. He also hoped that support for the Allied side could help shore up his tottering Beijing government with large-scale loans. From the Allied perspective, meanwhile, China was an invaluable source of manpower: Once Duan declared war, the Allies eagerly put tens of thousands of Chinese males to work at dockyards and construction sites in Western Europe to free up more European males for combat.

President Li objected strenuously to Duan's decision to declare war and much of the parliament agreed with him. Through a series of complex maneuvers, however, Duan was able to have Li replaced as president. Sun Yatsen, meanwhile, had long since entered the fray. Already, in January 1917, he had written an open telegram to British Prime Minister David Lloyd George that laid out his reasons for opposing China's entrance into the war. In the telegram, he bluntly stated that conflicts between whites were of little concern to the Chinese and he warned that antiforeignism—"Boxerism"—might reappear in China if it were dragged into the war against its will. Several months later, Sun sponsored a lengthy pamphlet titled *The Question of China's Survival* that expressed extreme hostility to Great Britain and treated Germany as effectually the lesser of two evils. In September 1917, Sun explained his reasoning to a Japanese reporter, "[W]e have no more love for Germany than for England, but from the standpoint of our national interests we do not want to see Germany beaten so completely that she will cease to be a restraining influence upon the British domination of the Far East." Given this anger at British domination, Japan's support for the Allied powers seriously disappointed Sun. As he told the reporter, "Your country is acting like a marionette on the British string." Sun had not forgotten that it was the British government that had propped up the regime of his archenemy, Yuan Shikai.

Sun's objections did not stop at words. In response to Duan's dictatorial actions and his insistence on bringing China into the war on the Allied side, Sun began to plan the creation of a rival Chinese government in the city of Guangzhou. His Shanghai underworld contacts had connections with the Chinese navy that enabled him to enlist the Naval Minister in his project. After laying the necessary groundwork, he traveled to Guangzhou and convinced the warlords there to allow him to set up his rival government. Next, he responded to the crisis that the Beijing parliament faced. The parliament had first been elected in 1912–1913 but had been dissolved during Yuan's dictatorship. Although it resumed its meetings after Yuan's death, more recent circumstances in Beijing had brought about its dissolution a second time. As Duan would not permit it to convene again in Beijing, Sun invited its members to Guangzhou to meet there instead. Before long, 130 representatives—one-third of the total parliament—had reached Guangzhou. In addition to the parliament, Sun invited the Chinese navy, which arrived in Guangzhou with 15 aging ships.

With a rump parliament (one-third of the parliament was legally insufficient for a quorum) and a modicum of naval protection, Sun could claim that he was preserving China's republican government and that a branch of the military recognized the legitimacy of his actions.

Where did Sun obtain the money for all of this? It was expensive, after all, to operate naval ships and to pay the travel and living expenses of so many members of parliament. The answer seems to be: German government agents. There is documentary evidence that Sun had made contact with the German consulate between March and August 1917 and that he had requested money from Germany. Separate evidence—the claim of a Guangdong warlord in August 1917—suggests that he indeed received a large sum, which would have gone toward the cost of creating the new government. Although the evidence is not incontestable, it is quite plausible that German agents would have been interested in Sun: He was loudly anti-British and Germany was looking anywhere it could for allies. It is equally plausible that Sun would have been interested in Germany, given his opposition to Great Britain and his eagerness for any assistance that could give him a toehold of power. The result was a very transitory marriage of convenience.

Indeed, the marriage was barely even a honeymoon. Scarcely had Sun begun to establish his Guangzhou government before he and an assistant visited the American consul in Guangzhou and announced to him that their government wanted to make war on Germany! Sun asked for American funding for his government and promised preferential treatment for American businesses—such as builders of military arsenals—in Guangzhou in return. The U.S. government did not take up the offer, and indeed, no foreign government recognized Sun's tiny government as the legitimate government over China. Nevertheless, the entire episode is revealing. First, Sun's overall hostility toward the Allies during World War I had lasting negative effects on his cause, inasmuch as it caused American officials and media outlets to regard him henceforth with deep suspicion. Second, his quick turnaround after he received funding from Germany—if indeed he had received funds—displays the essential opportunism and desperation that characterized his machinations during this period of his life. Sun had long maintained a habit of identifying his own fortunes with China's and this habit led him to justify virtually any action that benefited him as a necessary step toward the salvation of his country.

Sun's Guangzhou government was a very limited affair both geographically and temporally. He did accept the military title of grand marshal and he did dress the part, with gilded epaulettes, festoons of braid, white gloves, and so on. In reality, however, he had very little power. His government's offices were located in a concrete factory and many of his orders never extended very far beyond the factory.

Crucial to what little success he did experience was his alliance with **Chen Jiongming**, a reformist warlord who had participated in the 1911 revolution and anti-Yuan movements. Partially to protect Chen's forces from the attacks of a rival warlord, Sun gave Chen a base in Fujian province along China's southeast coast. While Sun hoped that Chen could use this base to conquer an increasing share of south and central China, his forces were simply too small. Nevertheless, this was the first time that Sun had spoken openly of a **"Northern Expedition"**—a broad military campaign northward—that could ultimately bring about the unification of China. Sun's plan of action displayed his primary intent in creating the government in Guangzhou: He wished to use it as a base for bringing *all* of China under the military control of his supporters. In the early 1920s, Sun would establish two successive governments, again in Guangzhou, and at some point during the existence of each of those governments, he would attempt a Northern Expedition. Following his death in 1925, the GMD would undertake a Northern Expedition on a vastly expanded scale and this time it would succeed in uniting virtually all of China beneath its rule.

Meanwhile, Sun's first Guangzhou government had little to show for itself. In May 1918, the major warlords of the region, the navy, and the rump parliament all agreed to reorganize the government, creating a directory of seven members to replace the single grand marshal. Although Sun was appointed as a member of the directory, he rejected the appointment and instead left for Japan. Following a short period there, he traveled to Shanghai, where he would spend the next two-and-a-half years writing books that illuminate his vision of a newer China.

Sun and the May Fourth Movement

While warlords sparred over Beijing and Sun Yatsen himself played the warlord in China's far south, a social and cultural movement emerged in China that would affect the country for decades and continues to shape aspects of Chinese experience even today. This is the **May Fourth Movement**, named after a political confrontation that took place in Beijing on May 4, 1919. The larger movement, however, began several years earlier and was originally called the New Culture movement. The movement took shape in a very special atmosphere in China's coastal cities in the mid-1910s that combined a sense of crisis with an underlying optimism. The crisis was the warlordism into which China had fallen. No viable political structures had replaced the Qing dynasty and the advent of warlordism amply underscored the resulting deficits in national unity and personal safety. The optimism of the period, in turn, derived from rapid industrial growth in the cities. This growth was creating new professions unconnected with traditional Chinese life that enabled many youth—prominently including females—to escape their elders' values and control for the very first time. The potent combination of national crisis and incipient individual liberation led increasing numbers of Chinese youth to conclude that China's problems required a cultural rather than a political solution. Specifically, they held that it was the persistence of "feudal" family structures that prevented China from achieving genuine modernization.

The flagship magazine of the movement was called *New Youth*, a title that neatly pairs together the two most popular buzzwords of the day. The great theme of this magazine was rebellion against Confucian tradition in all its forms, as summarized in the slogan "Overthrow Confucius and Sons." Who would replace Confucius? An especially famous essay that appeared in *New Youth* in

1919 stated that what China most needed was the presence of two gentlemen, Mr. Science and Mr. Democracy. Without them, many youth believed, China could never progress nor could it become strong and respected in the modern world.

The storm center of the movement was Beijing University, which in the 1910s promoted a wide-ranging discussion regarding China's future. Much of this discussion took a literary shape, as students devoured the works of innovative Chinese writers writing in vernacular Chinese—the language people actually spoke—rather than in the classical language long employed by scholars. Students aggressively promoted this new habit of writing in the vernacular and over time they succeeded in convincing publishers and educators, too, to reject the classical language as old-fashioned and impractical.

Despite the movement's focus on transforming Chinese culture, the immediate issue that gives the May Fourth Movement its name was indeed political. As we have seen, early in World War I the Japanese military captured German possessions in Shandong province. After the war ended in November 1918, many Chinese hoped that this strategically located province would be returned to China. However, while the war still raged, Japanese diplomats had already concluded secret agreements with several European powers that obligated those nations to support Japanese claims to Shandong. Moreover, Japanese officials had arranged a secret deal with Duan Qirui's Beijing government in September 1918 that permitted Japan to retain extensive rights in Shandong in return for a very large loan. The Japanese government was thus well positioned for the postwar peace conference that would resolve the many territorial issues arising out of World War I.

That peace conference took place in Versailles, France, from January to June of 1919. "China"—in other words, the Beijing government—sent a 62-member delegation to the conference. The delegates had ambitiously hoped to roll back the many privileges that Westerners enjoyed in their country. Instead, they were shocked to discover that the European powers—and the United States along with them—intended to allow Japan to maintain its overall control of Shandong. Far from fulfilling its diplomatic agenda, then, the Chinese delegation found to its great disappointment that the conference would erode Chinese sovereignty even further.

The *coup de grâce* came when the Japanese government revealed its secret September 1918 agreement with Duan's Beijing government that gave it special rights in Shandong. Japan, the Western powers, and China's own government all appeared to be collaborating to deprive China of what rightfully belonged to it! Having reached this conclusion, many of China's college students translated their anger into action: On May 4, 1919, 3,000 of them staged an angry demonstration at Tiananmen Square opposing the decision of the **Versailles Conference** to allow Japan to retain Shandong. In succeeding days, a general strike quickly spread among students and businesspeople, with protests breaking out in dozens of cities across China and a large-scale boycott of Japanese goods and services gathering steam.

In diplomatic terms, the effect of all of this turmoil was to convince the Chinese delegation not to sign the Versailles Treaty, which left the Shandong issue unsettled until the Japanese government relinquished control several years later. By far the greatest significance of the whole episode, however, was the impetus it gave to youthful mass nationalism in twentieth-century China. Henceforth, "new culture" would entail a new politics as well.

Sun Yatsen's response to the May Fourth Movement was very mixed. Historians writing from the GMD and Chinese Communist perspectives have sought to present his response to the movement as favorable. Both the revived GMD and the CCP received much of their initial vitality in the 1920s from the May Fourth Movement, predisposing them to assess it positively. By the same token, both parties also revere Sun Yatsen, inasmuch as he founded one of the parties and lent indispensable assistance to the other one. As a result, the two parties have a vested interest in describing Sun as having supported the movement.

Sun did make positive comments about the May Fourth Movement in two contexts. One context was a telegram that he and several other figures sent to the Beijing government in May 1919 to criticize the government's arrest of student protestors. While the telegram argued that the students "should be excused," however, it provided little elaboration, instead focusing most of its attention on attacking the government. The other, potentially more convincing, source of positive comments was a message that Sun sent to his overseas followers in January 1920. The message praises the New Culture Movement, stating that if its efforts continue, "the achievements are bound to be imposing, enduring, and far-reaching. The success of the revolution which our party desires to see accomplished will have to depend upon [such] a general reorientation of thought." However enthusiastic Sun may sound in this oft-quoted document, historian Y. C. Wang points out that Sun wrote the message solely to appeal for contributions to a proposed publishing house and English-language journal. Most of the message concentrated on those proposals rather than on the May Fourth Movement. Indeed, he appears to have referred to the movement primarily because he knew that it had inspired widespread enthusiasm and he wanted to tap into that enthusiasm for his own purposes.

One other piece of evidence that Sun agreed with the movement or at least adjusted his own rhetoric to match it was that he subsequently criticized the Japanese government more harshly in his statements. Aside from this, the bulk of the evidence suggests that Sun did not like the May Fourth Movement very much. Historians Sidney H. Chang and Leonard H. D. Gordon have described two major differences between Sun's nationalism and that of the students: (1) the students were vehemently anti-imperialist while Sun was quite willing to compromise with the imperialists in the short term in order to strengthen China in the long term, and (2) the students wanted to create a mass movement, while Sun sought to train a small elite that would seize power from the Beijing government. The greater idealism of the students as compared with Sun comes across in both cases: The students believed that China could manage without special foreign assistance and they believed that a mass movement could rapidly bring about a democratic China. Overall, Sun saw the students as naive. He expressed this view in a 1924 speech in which he disdainfully remarked, "They really do not know what revolution is."

Equally important, Sun disagreed with the students' assessment of traditional Chinese culture. While they hated it, he idealized it and regarded it as a necessary springboard for China's future achievements. In line with this view, Sun opposed the shift from classical to vernacular language and persisted in writing in classical Chinese even after most authors had abandoned it. Sun also felt that the students misunderstood the very Western culture that they idealized. He expressed this criticism in one of his 1924 lectures on the Three People's Principles:

> The liberty which Westerners talk about has its strict limitations and cannot be described as belonging to everyone. When young Chinese students talk about liberty, they break down all restraints. Because no one welcomes their theory in the society outside, they can only bring it back into their schools, and constant disorders result. This is abuse of freedom.

In short, while Sun shared with the students a fierce desire to build a strong, modern China, he disagreed with them on many points as to how that goal should be achieved.

Sun's Writings at the Rue Molière

Still another reason that Sun Yatsen did not become heavily involved in the May Fourth Movement was that he had become something of a recluse. In June 1918, he and his wife moved into a Western-style house on the Rue Molière in the French Concession of Shanghai. From then until December 1920, he focused most of his attention on writing two books, titled *Memoirs of a Chinese Revolutionary* and *The International Development of China*, respectively. Each of these books expressed Sun's strong faith that China would ultimately become a great modern nation despite the seemingly endless problems it faced at the end of the 1910s.

Let us examine these works briefly, beginning with Sun's second and more complex book, *The International Development of China*. As Sun had served as the salesman of the revolution in earlier years, so in this work he now acted as a salesman hawking China's markets and resources. In both the preface and the conclusion of the book, Sun argued that if the world were to suffer another world war like that which had just taken place, it would take shape as a violent struggle over control of the Chinese market. However, the future did not need to be so grim. Late in the war, European countries were producing tremendous quantities of goods used for all aspects of the combat. The war having since ended, these countries now needed what Sun called a "dumping ground" for their overproduction—a role for which China was ideally suited. Western factories that had produced cannons could now produce steam rollers for building Chinese roads, while Western factories that had produced tanks could now produce trucks for transporting Chinese raw materials. International cooperation could eliminate the need for a destructive trade war, rendering China a "New World in the economic sense." In actuality, the major combatants of World War I continued to reel from its effects. They focused sharply on the rebuilding of Europe and paid little attention to the economic development of other areas of the world. Sun could dream, however, and his dreams were in some cases prophetic.

The International Development of China consists of six economic programs that showcase Sun's sheer ambition as a planner of China's future. Much of the text consists of a meticulous description of his plans to integrate China by linking its many cities through railways, roads, dredged rivers, and so on. Central to the plans were two giant new port cities that he wanted to see constructed along China's east coast: one near Tianjin in north China and the other south of Shanghai. Each city, he predicted, would grow to be the size of New York City owing to the commerce that railways linking the ports to points west would generate.

Sun also turned his attention to China's huge rivers. Writing of the Yangzi in particular, he predicted that with proper dredging both banks of this river would "become two continuous cities" all the way from Shanghai to the metropolis of Wuhan some 600 miles upstream. Still further upriver, the Yangzi passes through a set of three famous gorges that in the early twentieth century could only be navigated by small boats. Sun's recommendation was that "the rapids should be dammed up to form locks to enable crafts to ascend the river as well as to generate water power." What he is advocating in this passage is what the PRC has recently constructed: the Three Gorges Dam. This dam, which today comprises the largest hydroelectric project on earth, was first envisioned by Sun Yatsen in this book full of far-fetched plans.

In his conclusion to the book, Sun presented China as a land where class tensions between capitalists and laborers had not yet become acute. As still another bid to attract foreign investment, he asserted that in contrast to the West, "[o]ur laboring class . . . are living from hand to mouth and will therefore only be too glad to welcome any capitalist who would even put up a sweat shop to exploit them." This statement foreshadows the approach that the Chinese government has taken in recent decades to economic development, enabling China to become, in effect, the world's factory.

Prior to writing *The International Development of China*, Sun composed *Memoirs of a Chinese Revolutionary*, a book that expressed his voluntaristic outlook toward China's future. Generally speaking, voluntarism is a perspective that holds that the key to success in a given activity lies in intensely and persistently focusing one's willpower on one's objective. Such an employment of willpower is exactly what Sun recommended for twentieth-century China. According to him, numerous Chinese remained under the spell of the ancient Chinese notion that "actions are difficult, but knowledge is easy." Sun heartily disliked such a passive outlook and he attributed the failure of the 1911 revolution to its continued influence among those Chinese, who hesitated to embrace the changes necessary for the revolution to truly succeed. So far as he was concerned, a much more beneficial expression would be "knowledge is difficult, but actions easy." Action, in the sense of a wholehearted engagement with China's challenges, could work wonders and work them quickly.

How quickly? Sun believed that China had special advantages that enabled it to modernize more rapidly than many other nations. For example, China would be modernizing in an era in which science was already well developed. In addition, its sheer size in terms of territory, population, and natural resources would prove invaluable. Here, then, is his prediction:

> In order to become a Great Power, Japan took only fifty years in place of the hundred which were required by the United States of America. Consequently, if we base ourselves on these standards and relationships China can become a very powerful State if she concentrates on the work of her transformation for the space of, say, ten years. I think that this space is sufficient.

As he remarked in the preface to the book, when the Chinese finally become aware of the task of reconstructing China that lay ahead of them, it will turn out to be "just as easy as the turning of a hand or the breaking of a twig."

While Sun's voluntarism was especially fervent, Sun was not the only writer in early twentieth-century China to combine frustration over China's weakness with a faith in its ultimate strength. In 1919, the same year that Sun published *Memoirs of a Chinese Revolutionary*, the young Mao Zedong published a piece titled "The Great Union of Popular Masses" in a journal in Hunan province. At age 26, Mao was not yet a Communist but he was already searching for radical solutions to China's problems. Expressing an outlook that he maintained with modifications even after he became China's leader, Mao declared, "We must know that the affairs of this world are, in themselves, very easy to deal with. If there are cases when they are not easy to deal with, that is because of the difficulties caused by the force of history—habit. If we can only give a shout together, we will shatter this force of history." Numerous political differences and a wide generation gap separated Sun Yatsen from Mao Zedong. In spite of this, Sun, had he known of it, would have fully agreed with Mao's expression of confidence in the power of the human will.

12

The South Gains Soviet Help

The time-spans of Sun Yatsen's three Guangzhou governments—1917–1918, 1920–1922, and 1923–1925—together comprise the last phase of his life. With Yuan dead and the warlord period underway, Sun now embraced a "southern strategy" to reunify China under his own rule by developing the southern city of Guangzhou as a base and then setting out on Northern Expeditions to conquer the rest of the country. As we have seen, the first Guangzhou government achieved little besides arousing the suspicions of the various major combatants in World War I. His second Guangzhou government would accomplish somewhat more insofar as it heralded Sun's son's efforts to modernize the city of Guangzhou. However, it too would collapse in the face of regional opposition, much as though Sun were a garden-variety warlord. The third Guangzhou government, on the other hand, would establish Sun's permanent place in modern Chinese history. Even as he continued to face serious local opposition, his alliance with the newly established Soviet Union would substantially alter the political and military equation for early twentieth-century China and would provide the institutional basis for the preservation and embellishment of his memory down to our own day. His southern strategy may not have succeeded within his lifetime in reunifying China, but it guaranteed that his aims and repute would far outlast those of his warlord adversaries.

Following the failure of his first Guangzhou government, Sun spent more than two years at the Rue Molière in Shanghai composing *Memoirs of a Chinese Revolutionary* and *The International Development of China*, the works discussed in Chapter 11. He also did something else. On October 10, 1919—the eighth anniversary of the overthrow of the Qing dynasty—Sun relaunched the Zhonghua Guomindang (Chinese Nationalist Party). Since 1913, Sun had served as the leader of the Chinese Revolutionary Party, which he created in the wake of his failure to remove Yuan Shikai from office following Yuan's apparent assassination of Song Jiaoren. That party, as we recall, was highly authoritarian and required a personal oath to Sun from all of its members. As the party never gained much support, in 1919, Sun reverted back to both the earlier name and the looser structure for a party that would implement his vision of a powerful modern China. From 1919 onward, the GMD remained operational for the remainder of Sun's life. Indeed, it has continued to play a central role in the politics of "Greater China"—the portion of East Asia in which ethnic Chinese predominate—well into the twenty-first century.

Sun's Second Guangzhou Government

The story of Sun's second government in the southern city of Guangzhou is inextricably linked to Chen Jiongming, a southern warlord who generally followed Sun's lead during the 1910s. It was Chen whom Sun rewarded in 1917, when he created his first Guangzhou government, by giving him a small army and a piece of territory in the coastal province of Fujian. By 1920, Chen had greatly expanded this army, still based in Fujian. Late in that year, Sun ordered him to attack the warlords of Guangdong province—the site of Guangzhou—and Chen complied. Chen's army rapidly defeated the Guangdong warlords, permitting Sun to establish the second of his three Guangzhou governments.

Perhaps Sun's most important act during the rule of his second Guangzhou government—December 1920 to June 1922—was that of appointing his son Sun Fo as mayor of Guangzhou. Sun Fo's extensive American education convinced him that Guangzhou needed to be organized along the lines of a modern Western city. This led him to take a number of steps during his years (1921–1925) as mayor: Besides creating an elected municipal council, he also introduced extensive new programs in such fields as public utilities, public health, road construction, and coeducational schooling. These changes were unprecedented for a Chinese city and transformed Guangzhou into a model for other coastal Chinese cities. Indeed, Guangzhou's attraction went further: The city rapidly became a mecca for educated radicals from all over China. As historian Ming Chan states, Guangzhou in the early 1920s served as "a real-life laboratory for anarchists, missionaries, anti-imperialists, socialists, reformers, and unionists . . ." In effect, it had become the epicenter of the search for a newer China.

Even as Guangzhou increasingly turned its face to the future, it served as a major center of resistance to the northern warlords, one or another alliance of whom was ruling over Beijing at any given time. As Sun himself wanted to rule over Beijing and China as a whole, his government alternately threatened and negotiated with the various alliances that struggled for power in the north. True to form, Sun also sought foreign aid. At the beginning of the 1920s, he pinned many of his hopes on the United States, which had triumphed in World War I and which he admired overall. However, in late 1921 and early 1922, the United States sponsored the **Washington Conference**, which brought together the major naval powers of the Pacific Ocean to resolve issues associated with the region. The Chinese delegation at the conference—representing the northern warlords—argued strongly for the abrogation of the "unequal treaties" and met the usual Western rebuff. Despite this failure, the nations at the conference definitively extended their recognition to the northern Chinese government as the sole legitimate government of China. It was as though Sun and his Guangzhou government did not exist.

Sun noticed, however, that certain powerful nations did not attend the Washington conference. In particular, there were no representatives from Germany, which had lost World War I, or Russia, which as the world's first Communist state opposed the Western capitalist nations. Moreover, while representatives from Japan did attend, the agreements signed at the conference were mostly unfavorable to them. Sun began to think that an alliance between his government and those of Germany, Russia, and Japan—outcasts all within the world order of the 1920s— might be a good idea. He sought contact with these nations' diplomats and offered his usual outlandish promises to attract them to his proposed alliance. As we will see later in this chapter, the one nation that would eventually take up his offer—with far-reaching consequences—was Russia.

Meanwhile, we need to return to Chen Jiongming, Sun's warlord ally. After Sun returned to Guangzhou in 1920, he appointed Chen as the civil governor of Guangdong province. However, Sun and Chen soon clashed. The immediate issue was that Sun was again eager to conquer northern China through a Northern Expedition. During his first Guangzhou government, as we have seen, Sun used the province of Fujian as his base of operations. This time, he used Guilin, a strikingly beautiful city in nearby Guangxi province, as his base. Chen, however, sharply rejected Sun's plan to conquer China: He felt both that Sun lacked the troops to accomplish such a giant task and that conquering China, itself, was the wrong way to reunify the country. Chen favored something called "federalism," a popular notion among some warlords in the early 1920s. The federalists agreed that China needed greater political unity. However, they felt that the process of creating such unity should be gradual and peaceful and that even after reunification China's individual provinces should retain autonomy over matters that concerned them alone. From this perspective, Chen believed that the best way Guangdong could contribute to the future unification of China was by developing itself as a model province rather than by conquering other provinces. Accordingly, he refused to contribute much money or many troops to Sun's operation in Guilin. In response, in April 1922, Sun fired Chen from his post as governor, paving the way for a confrontation.

After Sun's troops in Guilin failed to achieve results, some of them withdrew toward Guangdong province. Chen's troops, likewise in Guangdong, feared that their wages would be eliminated now that Sun was hostile to Chen. As tensions grew, Sun ordered Chen's troops to leave Guangzhou, stating, "People often say that I am a 'boasting big gun [*Sun dapao*, Sun's derogatory nickname].' Well, this time there will be a real 'big gun.' If they . . . refuse to obey my order, I shall use conical shells or eight-inch guns with poison-gas shells, which can easily finish them off in three hours." Chen's chief lieutenant responded by plotting to have Sun forcibly removed from office.

Soong Qingling later published a dramatic description of the events that transpired once Chen's lieutenant's plot had been set into motion. Her story starts at the point at which Chen's troops surrounded the Presidential Palace:

> About two o'clock on the morning of June 16 Dr. Sun roused me from my sweet dreams, telling me to hurry and dress, that we were in danger and must escape. . . . I thought it would be inconvenient for him to have a woman along

with him, and urged him to leave me behind for the time being. . . . At last he saw the sense of my argument, but he would not go even then until he had left all fifty of our bodyguard to protect the house . . . The enemy fired downhill at us from two sides, shouting 'Kill Sun Wen [i.e., Sun Yatsen]! Kill Sun Wen!'. . . . As day broke our men began to reply to the fire with their rifles and machine guns, while the enemy employed field guns. . . . By eight o'clock our store of ammunition was running low . . . Our captain advised me to leave and the troops agreed with him, promising for their part to stay there in order to halt any possible pursuit by the enemy. . . . Later, all of the fifty were reported killed.

Through a series of further misadventures, Qingling was eventually able to escape to Hong Kong by disguising herself as a peasant woman. Qingling, pregnant at the time of these events, wound up having a miscarriage and losing her only opportunity to have a child with Sun.

Sun himself had meanwhile escaped to a loyal warship that was docked in Guangzhou harbor. Within days, he was joined on the ship by Qingling and by his lieutenant Chiang Kaishek, who henceforth became his close advisor. Sun waited on the ship for more of his troops in Guilin to reach Guangzhou and extricate him from his predicament. They never arrived, however, and in August he gave up, traveling first to Hong Kong and then to Shanghai. This marked the end of his second Guangzhou government. Chen's troops had gained control over the city and as part of their revenge on Sun they destroyed his collection of personal papers, a record thereby lost to historians.

Subsequent generations of Chinese have almost universally supported Sun in his confrontation with Chen Jiongming. It is worth remembering, however, that this was not a pure power struggle. Chen disagreed in principle with Sun's nearly obsessive focus on a Northern Expedition as the way to bring peace to China. He also objected to the heavy taxes that Sun's government had imposed on businesses in Guangzhou in order to pay for this quixotic expedition. Moreover, some of Sun's methods tend to be forgotten by the GMD and CCP historians who portray the Sun–Chen struggle. The day after Sun escaped to his warship, he gathered a squadron of additional warships from a nearby location and ordered the squadron to bomb the city of Guangzhou. This largely indiscriminate bombardment reportedly caused the deaths of more than a hundred civilians. When one of Sun's generals protested his action, Sun told him, "We have to do it to improve our position in negotiations [with Chen]." Within the brutal environment of intra-warlord fighting in the early 1920s, Sun was willing to become yet another brute if he felt it could help him unify and strengthen China. He was not motivated by material greed, as many warlords were, but his idealism and self-confidence did have their violent edge.

The Russian Connection

To understand the next stage of Sun's career, we need to step back temporarily from the scene in southern China for a much wider view of the early twentieth century. Specifically, we need to turn to the world of ideas, where a new conception of world history was arousing fervent hopes and equally fervent resistance.

This conception of world history, Marxism, presented itself as a comprehensive explanation of the modern world and its future direction. Named after nineteenth-century German revolutionary Karl Marx, its central argument was that history comprised a series of ascending evolutionary stages. Starting with ancient slavery, these would move through feudalism and capitalism to arrive at socialism—and communism as socialism's highest form. According to Marxists, as advanced capitalist nations approached their socialist tipping point, a radical overthrow of their institutions could bring about a more equitable and fulfilling society. Such a perspective had subsisted for decades on the margins of European intellectual life. However, it came to the fore with the success of the Communist revolution in Russia in 1917, which convinced some observers that Marxism was indeed the wave of the future.

It is worth appreciating the sheer radicalism and idealism of the Marxist outlook because of its importance to the last several years of Sun Yatsen's political career. Sun himself never adopted a Marxist perspective—his socialism, as we have seen, was quite mild and was heavily admixed with an appreciation of capitalist dynamism. However, his eagerness for foreign aid would lead him to ally his GMD with the Soviet Union, which meant that Soviet aid, Soviet advice, and Soviet-backed Chinese Communists flowed into his party. The effects of this on Sun, his party, and the history of twentieth-century China would be immense.

We need to be clear about terminology: While *Marxism* was the theory about world history, the political movement to bring individual societies to an advanced form of socialism was called *Communism* (and where the movement succeeded, the governments it established were likewise labeled Communist). In Russia—soon renamed the Soviet Union—the leader of the new Communist government was a professional revolutionary named **Vladimir Lenin**. For the first three years after the revolution in 1917, the Russian government under Lenin concentrated on defeating its foes—supporters of the previous czarist regime—in a prolonged civil war. During the war, Lenin hoped that the peoples of Europe would join his Communist revolution because he believed that this would help raise the world as a whole to a new stage of development. As matters transpired, however, his success in defeating his Russian enemies was not matched by success in spreading the revolution beyond Russia's borders.

It was at this juncture that Lenin created the Communist International, usually abbreviated as the **"Comintern."** This organization, begun in 1919, sought to spread the Communist revolution throughout the world by undermining existing governments. Initially, it concentrated its attention on Europe. However, by the time the second congress of the Comintern met in 1920, it had become clear that European governments were too powerful to be overthrown directly. In light of this, Lenin set forth his "Theses on the National and Colonial Questions." This document, which set the policy for the congress, stipulated that Communists should ally themselves with national independence movements among colonized nations, even if those movements were not socialist or Communist. The strategy was to infiltrate such movements—which after all could gather support on nationalistic grounds—and then take them over as they approached success. Lenin viewed this as a "flank attack" on Western capitalism at its weakest point:

the colonies on which it relied for its growth. He was especially interested in India—Britain's largest colony—and China—a semicolony shared among the Western powers. As both nations were located in Asia, he asserted that "[t]he East will help us to conquer the West."

Lenin's theses envisioned a specific relationship between the Communists and the national independence movements. First, any alliance with such a movement needed to be temporary—it was a means to attain Communist control. Second, Communists needed to build up their own independent strength even while an alliance continued. Third and finally, Communists needed to give special support to any peasant movements that had organized against landlord rapacity—still another issue that Communists could use for their own purposes. These three features are highly significant for our story because *all* of them became hallmarks of the alliance that the Soviet Union established with Sun Yatsen and his GMD in 1923.

In the wake of the radical May Fourth Movement of 1919, both Marxism and the Soviet Union were receiving favorable attention among members of China's educated elite. In part, this owed to the fact that Marxism set forth universal principles (as Confucianism had done), promised swift modernization, and presented a reassuring global harmony as its final goal. The favorable impression that the Soviet Union itself garnered, however, was primarily created by a single act: In 1919, a high-ranking Russian official announced that his government rejected the special privileges that Russians had previously enjoyed under the "unequal treaties." The actual situation was less clear-cut, as Russian diplomats quickly negotiated treaties with northern warlords that restored some of the privileges that their government had renounced. Regardless, the move was a stroke of genius from a public relations standpoint: It could not have contrasted more sharply with the Western powers' rigid insistence at the Versailles Conference on maintaining their customary privileges in China. As a result, Soviet representatives could expect at least a sympathetic ear as they made a series of efforts in the 1920s to influence Chinese affairs.

One step that Soviet agents took to influence China was to set up the Chinese Communist Party (CCP) in Shanghai in 1921. At least initially, however, the CCP was tiny and had no prospect of achieving power over China. As Soviet agents attempted to foster the CCP's growth, then, they also took other steps to expand their impact on Chinese politics.

Casting their net widely, Soviet diplomats in the early 1920s contacted anyone and everyone whom they perceived as powerful in China. They held talks with the government in Beijing, met with individual warlords outside of the government, and touched base with Sun Yatsen as well. The Soviet Union had several objectives: to create a buffer against an expansionist Japan, avoid being encircled by pro-Western governments, and utilize China as a means to subvert the British colonial government in India. In any case, China's fluid political situation and rising nationalist sentiment encouraged Soviet leaders to believe that their country could gain substantial influence there.

In 1921 and 1922, several Comintern agents visited Sun. Most of them were discouraged by Sun's overwhelming emphasis on a military solution to China's problems: He habitually insisted that China needed to be conquered before any social reforms could be contemplated. The Soviets saw this as putting the cart before the horse, inasmuch as they held that propaganda—the trumpeting of reforms—was essential before any conquest could succeed. Despite this disagreement, an agent code-named Maring concluded after meeting with Sun that he was the figure with whom the Soviet Union should ally. As a result, when the Soviet Union sent one of its senior diplomats, Adolf Joffe, to Beijing in 1922, it instructed Joffe to contact Sun as well and to conclude an alliance if possible.

Joffe's negotiations with Sun in late 1922 bore fruit in a joint statement that the two figures issued in January 1923. The format of the statement was that of an agreement between high-ranking government officials from two countries—the first official foreign recognition that Sun had received. The actual text concentrated on issues that had divided the Soviet and Beijing governments and incorporated Sun's view that Communism was inappropriate for China. What was more important, however, was that the very existence of the statement publicly signaled a friendship between the Soviet Union on the one hand and the GMD on the other. From this point on, the friendship—or, more accurately, the strategic alliance—would deepen.

The "United Front" Alliance

Neither Sun nor Joffe regarded their joint statement as a commitment to an exclusive long-term relationship. Thus, on the very day that Sun signed the statement, he sent off a telegram seeking American aid in reunifying China peacefully. In like manner, Soviet diplomats kept their door wide open to other Chinese power-holders. Something new had nevertheless begun.

While Sun and Joffe were conferring in the fall of 1922, the GMD and the CCP were ironing out the specifics of their upcoming alliance. The agreement that they reached was that members of the CCP would be permitted to join the GMD—by far the larger of the two parties—but that they would have to join as individuals and submit themselves to the authority of the GMD as long as they remained members. In effect, each side was seeking to use the other: The GMD wanted Soviet aid, while the CCP wanted to participate in a larger and better known organization that shared at least its nationalistic goals. At the same time, it is important to realize that some members of each party were very reluctant about the alliance. GMD conservatives—including Sun's son Sun Fo—preferred to see their party align itself with Western capitalist nations. Meanwhile, a number of CCP members feared that an alliance with the GMD would dilute their radical Communist message. These misgivings would last throughout the life-span of the alliance, which extended two years beyond Sun's death in 1925.

So long as Sun was a leader without a functioning government, the alliance was a theoretical prospect anyway. However, in early 1923, Sun was able to establish his third and final Guangzhou government as a result of a new set of circumstances. Since the late 1910s, a large body of soldiers from the southwest province of Yunnan lived and fought in Guangdong province. While they had originally been a united, disciplined fighting force, over the course of several years they split into numerous groups of mercenaries, each on sale to the highest bidder. In late 1922, Sun became that highest bidder, paying a number of them to drive Chen Jiongming's soldiers out of Guangzhou. When they succeeded at this mission the following year, Sun was able to establish his third and most important Guangzhou government. Over the next two years, the Soviet Union provided military aid and training that would enable Sun to build a loyal GMD army. In the meantime, the Yunnanese—along with a large cohort of bodyguards that included a notorious Canadian nicknamed "two-gun Cohen"—became his muscle as he struggled to hold Guangzhou together.

As part of the alliance, Sun and the Soviets agreed to a trade: Sun would send his lieutenant Chiang Kaishek to the Soviet Union for military training, while the Soviets would send a Comintern agent and other military personnel to Guangzhou to help reorganize the GMD. The agent whom the Soviets sent to Guangzhou was a Russian Jew known as **Mikhail Borodin** (his actual family name was Grusenberg). Borodin was an interesting choice: As an individual, he was friendly and relaxed rather than severe and intense as Russian revolutionaries were reputed to be. A lengthy residence in the United States had rendered him fluent in English and he had recently participated in Comintern assignments to Europe and Latin America. He knew very little about China at the time he arrived there. Surprisingly, this did not diminish his effectiveness: Borodin was able to work with a variety of people and he quickly realized that a close relationship with Sun would be vital to his success. Borodin and Sun soon began to have lengthy English-language conversations in Sun's garden as they plotted together to revitalize the GMD as a force in Chinese politics.

Shortly after Borodin arrived in Guangzhou in October 1923, Sun's government landed in severe trouble: Sun's hired Yunnanese guns were having enormous difficulty preventing Chen Jiongming's soldiers, encamped east of Guangzhou, from reconquering the city. Borodin quickly took control of the situation, organizing groups of volunteers to defend the city against Chen's forces. The strategy worked, saving the Guangzhou government from ruin. In response, from this time onward Sun began to call Borodin his "Lafayette" and to place a good deal—though never all—of his trust in him.

The degree of Sun's commitment to Borodin became apparent at the first nationwide GMD Congress, held in January 1924. Almost 200 delegates attended the Congress representing China's provinces and major overseas Chinese communities. Many of these delegates were perturbed by the expanding cooperation between their party and the Soviet Union. Nevertheless, Sun pushed successfully to have the Congress pass an anti-imperialist charter and to approve several Communists for inclusion in the Central Executive Committee. He also had the party reconfigured so that it possessed a pyramidal structure similar to that of the Soviet Communist Party. Significantly, it so happened that Lenin died on one of the days that the Congress was meeting. When word reached the Congress, it adjourned for 3 days as a gesture of respect and Sun gave an impassioned eulogy that praised Lenin as "exceptional."

Had Sun become a mere lackey of his Communist allies? In a word, no. He dearly sought the aid that the Soviet Union could provide and he was willing to alter aspects of his party in order to obtain it. He viewed the Russian Revolution as a success—in contrast to his own string of failures—and he wanted to copy those elements of the Soviet model which contributed to that success. In his view, the single most important factor in the triumph of the Soviet Communist Party was its tight hierarchical structure. Such a structure was actually something he had clumsily attempted to create with his Chinese Revolutionary Party in 1913, several years before he even became aware of the Communist model. In sum, the lessons that Sun took from Lenin were primarily organizational. Despite his facile equation of his third principle—people's livelihood—with "communism," he insisted on maintaining his own distinct outlook on China's future path.

Sun expressed this outlook at length in the 16 lectures he gave during 1924 on the Three People's Principles. We have already examined some of the contents of these lectures in our survey of his ideology in Chapter 6. We have not yet encountered the opinions he expressed regarding Marxism, however. In his first of four lectures on people's livelihood, Sun presented a critical view of Marxism that drew heavily on a book by American socialist Maurice William. Marxists, for their part, regard conflicts between social classes—class wars—very positively, arguing that they drive human societies to higher levels of development. Sun disagreed with this approach, stating, "Class war is not the cause of social progress, it is a disease developed in the course of social progress." As a result, "Marx can only be called a social pathologist . . ." Sun also asserted that "the facts of Western history, in the seventy-odd years since Marx, have directly contradicted his theory." To support this assessment, he turned to the Ford assembly line and the improvements it had brought to its workers:

> Marx said that the capitalist would have to lengthen the working-day; the Ford factories have shortened the working-day. Marx said that the capitalist would have to reduce wages; the Ford factories have raised wages. Marx said the capitalist would have to raise the price of the manufactured product; the Ford factories have reduced the price of their product.

This speech greatly angered Borodin, who engaged in a passionate debate with Sun over its contents afterward. Rattled by this response, Sun softened his criticisms of Marxism in subsequent lectures. Despite this, he continued to embrace socialism as a means of *reducing* conflicts between social classes rather than as a way of bringing such conflicts to a head.

Beyond the lectures on the Three People's Principles, there is still another point on which Sun resisted Borodin. Following Lenin's theses on colonialism, Borodin repeatedly pressured Sun to call for radical land reform in China's vast countryside. The land reform Borodin had in mind would have eliminated landlordism completely by distributing all agricultural land directly to the peasants who tilled it. Significantly, Sun consistently withstood Borodin's pressure on this point. While Sun did express concern regarding the abysmal living conditions of many peasants, he wanted to improve these conditions by introducing labor-saving machinery rather than by transforming the social structure of the countryside. Nevertheless, he did allow Communist members of the GMD to establish peasant associations that operated autonomously. Over the next several years, these increasingly radical associations were to grow tremendously in size and influence under the leadership of such youthful Communist firebrands as Mao Zedong.

The single most important practical result of the GMD–CCP alliance during Sun's lifetime was the creation of the **Huangpu Military Academy**. This academy was built on the site of an old fort located on an island 10 miles south of Guangzhou. The first commandant of the academy when it opened in mid-1924 was Chiang Kaishek, who by this time had returned from the Soviet Union. Interestingly, the vice director of political training at the academy was Zhou Enlai, a Communist who would later serve as China's prime minister during the first quarter-century after the Communist takeover in 1949. This is an example of the tangled personal relations between leaders of the GMD and the CCP: Chiang—later a fierce anti-Communist—and Zhou—later a leading Communist— would become archenemies, yet while the United Front lasted in the mid-1920s they worked side by side to strengthen the GMD. It is similar to the situation in the American Civil War, in which generals on opposing sides had earlier served together on the American side of the Mexican-American war.

When the Huangpu Military Academy first opened its doors, it had 500 cadets. With abundant assistance from the Soviet Union, the academy rapidly produced large numbers of well-trained officers who, in turn, provided the foundation for

Sun Yatsen, seated, with Chiang Kaishek standing behind him in 1924 at the opening of the Huangpu Military Academy. (*CORBIS/NY*)

an ever-expanding army. It was this army which accomplished the massive Northern Expedition in 1926–1928 that finally united China militarily under GMD rule. And it was certain members of this army who, rejecting the GMD as the United Front fractured during the Northern Expedition, created the basis for the CCP's Red Army (predecessor to today's People's Liberation Army). Overall, it is difficult to exaggerate the influence that Huangpu graduates would eventually have on the history of modern China.

Before we leave the topic of "Red Canton"—as Sun's enemies began to call Guangzhou—it is worth asking how Sun actually viewed his party's alliance with the Soviet Union. To answer this, it is important to recall that his years of appeals to Western governments for assistance had left him virtually empty-handed. One can detect his sense of relief in a remark he made in a late 1923 lecture at the Guangzhou YMCA: "We no longer look to the Western powers. Our faces are turned toward Russia." This did not mean that he liked or sought to adopt every aspect of the Russian model, only that he was tired of "crossing the desert," as a Sun biographer has phrased it. On one occasion in 1923, an American acquaintance asked him skeptically whether he viewed the Soviets as democratic. Sun immediately responded, "I do not care what they are if they are willing to back me against Peking [i.e., the Beijing government]." Despite this eagerness, Sun did not regard his party as a mere supplicant in its relation with the Soviet Union. On the contrary, he believed that his side held final control over the situation. As he stated candidly in a conversation with one of his aides, "We may merely yoke up Soviet Russia and mount it [like a horse]."

Sun's Underlying Impatience

Even as Sun was strengthening the GMD through its Soviet alliance, he could barely retain control over Guangzhou itself. Sun Fo's modernization schemes for the city required a great deal of money, as did salaries for the Yunnanese mercenaries who still patrolled the streets. Guangzhou's merchants were expected to pay for all of this and they did not like it. To deal with the situation, they did what merchants were doing in other cities across China, namely, create a self-defense force. This force, called the Guangzhou Merchant Corps, grew quickly, reaching an estimated 50,000 members by the summer of 1924. As the Corps displayed hostility to Sun's government, Sun began to seek ways to restrict its activities. Suspecting a link between the Corps and Chen Jiongming—whose forces were still based east of Guangzhou—Sun had his government seize a Norwegian vessel in Guangzhou harbor that carried weapons for the Corps.

Sun's action led to a months-long standoff in which the Corps threatened a general strike in the city and Sun declared martial law. At length, the two sides reached a compromise whereby Sun would return half of the confiscated guns. However, on the day the guns were to be returned in October 1924, a violent confrontation erupted between the two sides. Ensuing developments led Sun—with some advice from Borodin—to opt for destroying the Corps once and for all by setting the fortified Guangzhou business district on fire. As their very first mission, Huangpu cadets carried out this order, reducing dozens of city blocks to ashes and permanently eliminating the Corps as a threat. This fit Sun's larger pattern in the 1920s: As in his earlier conflict with Chen Jiongming, Sun was willing to be ruthless whenever his control over Guangzhou was at stake.

During September 1924, right while his conflict with the Corps was deepening, Sun made the startling move of leaving Guangzhou altogether and traveling with some mercenaries to the city of Shaoguan in northern Guangdong province. He was going to start another Northern Expedition! He wrote Chiang Kaishek to explain that the GMD faced too many pressures in Guangzhou for it to remain there. As it turned out, his attempted expedition did not amount to anything significant militarily and he soon returned to Guangzhou. Nevertheless, his abandonment of the city, however temporary, effectively displayed his underlying mind-set. Essentially, he did not want to wait for his party to become strong gradually through military training and propaganda. Rather, he preferred to take action—almost any action—in order to reassure himself that his cause was still on the move.

Sun's outlook in this regard contrasts strongly with that of a number of modern Asian revolutionaries, such as Mao Zedong, Mohandas Gandhi, and Ho Chi Minh. Whereas these revolutionaries used patience as one of their greatest weapons against their Western enemies, Sun sought quick results in everything he did. Thus, while he could impressively persevere in a single cause for years on end, he did so only because he continually believed that success lay just around the corner. Gradual processes—even that of party-building through a foreign alliance—could not sustain his interest for long.

Fortunately for Sun, he did not need to wait much after returning to Guangzhou before a new opportunity arose for him. Conditions had changed in northern China and at the beginning of November he received an invitation to participate in talks in Beijing regarding China's future government. On November 13, 1924, Sun Yatsen sailed away from Guangzhou, never to return.

13

Sun's Death and Beatification

Sun's departure from Guangzhou in November 1924 was prompted by a shift in the tangled warlord politics of northern China. Some two years earlier, the situation in the north had begun to stabilize, as an alliance headed by warlord Wu Peifu gained overall control over much of north and central China. This prompted a rival alliance based in Manchuria to await an opportunity to dislodge Wu. It found its chance at last in a massive confrontation in September 1924 (indeed, Sun's "Northern Expedition" of that month had aimed to defeat Wu's southern allies). Wu's alliance, initially favored, lost the battle when one of Wu's own generals betrayed him and chased him out of Beijing. This general—Feng Yuxiang—and his allies asked Duan Qirui to serve as the new president of the Beijing government. As Feng had long appreciated Sun's views, he invited him to Beijing to help organize a conference aimed at unifying China.

Sun was elated. He felt that if he could steer the conference in the direction of accepting his leadership, he might be able to bring China together without having to do so through conquest. Not surprisingly, he accepted the invitation. To win over various interested parties, however, he decided to travel to Beijing in stages, stopping along the way at Shanghai, Kobe (in Japan), and Tianjin. When he reached Shanghai, the leading British newspaper at the international settlement there called on settlement leaders to expel Sun. As British Hong Kong had long maintained frosty relations with Sun's Guangzhou governments, the sentiment was predictable. Sun, however, used the newspaper's remarks as an opportunity to lecture the British, reminding them that they were guests in China and warning them of serious consequences if the "unequal treaties" were maintained. Among nationally famous Chinese politicians, Sun was unique in adopting this sort of tone with Western nations and his popularity soared as a result.

Sun's next stop was Japan, where he hoped to obtain Japanese government support for his upcoming effort to unify China through negotiation. Unfortunately for him, the government preferred to deal with Duan Qirui's representatives, who were already in Tokyo. The Japanese public, on the other hand, was quite enamored with Sun, especially when he praised Japanese determination and criticized Western arrogance. While in Kobe, he gave a much-quoted speech advocating pan-Asianism, that is, the idea that Asian nations needed to work together to oppose Western imperialism on their continent. From a Soviet Communist standpoint, this was highly off-message: The Russian government feared right-wing Japan and did not want China to cooperate with it. While Sun agreed with the Soviet Union's opposition to Western imperialism, however, he saw no reason why Japan and China—and for that matter, Russia—could not oppose it together as fellow "Asiatics."

The pan-Asianist speech was one of the last that Sun ever gave. Two days afterward, he traveled by ship to Tianjin in northern China, arriving on December 4. Tianjin, as it happens, was where Sun's efforts to seek a newer China had had their start in 1894, when as a young man he delivered his letter of enthusiastic advice to the office of Li Hongzhang. Now, 30 years later, a large crowd greeted him and his wife at the Tianjin docks. He looked exhausted, however, and before long he had to take to a sickbed. As he lay ill, Duan Qirui himself came to visit him and discuss politics. The two figures sharply disagreed: Sun wanted China's prospective national government to renounce the "unequal treaties," while Duan wanted it to maintain good relations with Western nations in order to preserve their flow of aid. Sun and Duan had angry arguments—doubtless worsening Sun's condition—and Duan refused in the end to cooperate with Sun on organizing the conference.

At the end of December, Sun traveled to Beijing to seek medical treatment. Once again, a huge crowd of well-wishers greeted him. He proved to be too ill to address them, although he made a short speech—his last—at the Hotel de Pekin shortly afterward. To treat his condition, he was brought to the Beijing Union Medical College hospital, where he spent most of the month of January, 1925. He was soon informed that he had cancer and that it had spread to his liver. After operating on him late in the month, hospital personnel concluded that his malady had reached a stage where they could do little to help him. At this point, Sun accepted an invitation from Wellington Koo, China's leading diplomat, to spend his remaining days at his Beijing residence.

Now the politics began. By 1925, Sun had amassed a good deal of power: His party possessed an increasingly large and well-trained army, while his government maintained control over the southern metropolis of Guangzhou. He enjoyed a widespread reputation for integrity, with even Chinese who disliked his politics acknowledging that he was not corrupt in the manner of the warlords. Moreover, his anti-imperialist words and deeds had boosted his popularity among nationalistic urban Chinese. The question of the hour was what would happen to Sun's political capital once he himself departed from the scene. Who would succeed him? What would his legacy be as China continued on its path toward unity and power? Sun's diverse crew of associates lacked any shared vision as to what should happen next.

Indeed, their jockeying for position was viscerally evident near Sun's deathbed. For the most part, only Sun's relatives were allowed near Sun himself. Soong Qingling permitted regular access to Sun to just two outside figures: **Wang Jingwei**, a longstanding Cantonese aide, and Mikhail Borodin, the Comintern agent. Wang wrote a "Leader's Will" for Sun with the approval of a small coterie of GMD officials (the GMD would later claim that Sun dictated the will and

Wang merely transcribed it). The will was read to Sun in late February, although he only signed it on March 11, the day before his death. As the Leader's Will later became the centerpiece of GMD civil ritual—something like the American Pledge of Allegiance—it is worth quoting in part:

> For forty years I have devoted myself to the cause of the National Revolution, the object of which is to raise China to a position of independence and equality. The experience of these forty years has convinced me that, to attain this goal, the people must be aroused... The Revolution has not yet been successfully concluded. Let all our comrades follow my writings... and make every effort to carry them into effect....

After Sun signed the document on March 11—with Qingling guiding his shaking hand—nine other figures countersigned it. Shortly after Sun's death, it became for many Chinese the distilled expression of his life: In their view, Sun had struggled, ceaselessly and selflessly, for China and now it was time for a new generation to complete what he had begun.

There were other documents at Sun's bedside on March 11. One of them was a flowery letter of farewell to the government of Soviet Russia, written with Borodin's assistance. The letter dramatically depicts the Soviet Union and China as allies in a global struggle against imperialism and requests the Soviet Union's continued aid to the GMD. Significantly, no one countersigned the letter as a witness and it was not released to the Chinese press as the Leader's Will was. Aside from the public will and the letter, there was also a personal will that left Sun's possessions—his books, belongings, and house—to Qingling. The most striking feature of the personal will is that it shows just how little Sun possessed at the end. Although millions of dollars had passed through his hands during his lifetime—he never really stopped raising money—it had all been spent on his causes and virtually none of it had wound up in his own pocket.

How did Sun spend his final lucid moments? Here stories diverge considerably. Sterling Seagrave, author of a collective biography of the Soong sisters, has brought together several versions of what took place:

> Borodin claimed that Sun had the presence of mind to say, "If only the Russians continue to help..." Those who were anxious to placate the West claimed that he gasped, "Don't make trouble for the Christians..." Even those who were many miles away—like Chiang Kai-shek—laid claim to some final benediction. The ambitious commandant of Whampoa [i.e., Huangpu] Academy told everyone that Dr. Sun had used his last breath to pronounce the name "Chiang Kai-shek."

Adding to the confusion, the official version of the episode in the PRC is that Sun's last words were "Peace, struggle, save China..." As there were only a small number of witnesses at Sun's bedside and each of them had their vested interests, we may never find out what words, if any, he actually uttered during his final hours.

Sun Yatsen died at age 58 on the morning of March 12, 1925.

Sun's Beatification, Pre-1949

It often happens in history that the death of an influential figure triggers a rush of claims to that figure's legacy. This certainly occurred in Sun Yatsen's case. A number of Chinese began to interpret his life and work for political purposes immediately after he died and the process has continued ever since. The memory of Sun—almost invariably, the *selective* memory of Sun—remains a vital factor in Chinese politics in the twenty-first century.

The first, logical question that arose after Sun died was that of how to bury him. What sort of service should be held? Where should his body be placed? Sun's family wanted a Christian service while the GMD—and especially its Communist allies—wanted a political commemoration. In the end, both observances took place, with the Christian service coming first. The service was held in a chapel in Beijing, and it took alleged similarities between Sun and Jesus Christ as its primary theme. H. H. Kung, Soong Ailing's husband, told the mourners that Sun had confided before his death, "Just as Christ was sent by God to the world, so also did God send me." The main eulogy expanded on this theme of parallels with Jesus by quoting other statements by Sun: "He [i.e., Jesus] was a revolutionist; so am I." "He came to save the poor, and the unfortunate, and those in bondage. So have I also tried to do." "He decried the traditions maintained by the lawmakers of Judea, and pleaded for universal brotherhood. It is because of similar shackles that bind China that I have made my crusade. . . ." As the chapel was small, very few people actually heard when these statements by Sun were repeated at the service. However, thousands waiting outside witnessed Sun's coffin being carried away after the ceremony was over.

Next, it was the Soviets' turn. The coffin was brought to "Central Park"—later renamed Zhongshan Park—in downtown Beijing, where it lay in state for three weeks as several hundred thousand Chinese filed by. The coffin was made of glass with Sun visible inside, dressed in a Western suit and partially covered by a GMD flag. Phonograph records played at high volume filled the air with Sun's own voice proclaiming the Three People's Principles. Befitting the Soviet motif, the Russian ambassador to the Beijing government was conspicuously represented among the mourners.

Three weeks of public mourning were followed by a provisional burial in Beijing. Sun had stated before his death that he wanted to be buried on Purple Mountain outside Nanjing in the vicinity of the early Ming emperors. While this would eventually take place, it required resources that the GMD did not have in 1925. Consequently, the decision was made to emplace Sun for the time being at the Azure Cloud Temple in a Beijing suburb. Sun's body was transferred to a Chinese-style heavy wood coffin, carried to the temple in a large procession, and ceremonially installed in a high chamber. There he would remain for four years as political developments swirled out of control, shattering the alliance he created and forging a newly unified China under GMD rule.

During his final years, Sun Yatsen had never appointed anyone to succeed him as GMD party chief. The most likely candidate for the position was Wang Jingwei, who had worked closely with Sun both before the 1911 revolution and during the three Guangzhou governments. At a formal level, the second national GMD Congress, held in early 1926, decided that the position of *zongli*—leader—would be accorded forever to Sun as no one could truly fill his shoes. Nevertheless, the GMD needed at least a de facto leader and Wang seemed well qualified as he maintained a good reputation among both leftists and rightists within the party. Chiang Kaishek, however, commanded the party's growing army and in 1926 he was able to outmaneuver Wang and establish himself as Sun's political successor. As noted in Chapter 10, Chiang would propose to and marry Soong Meiling, sister of Qingling, in the following year to signal that he was at some level Sun's familial heir as well. This decision, in turn, reinforced his massive Northern Expedition, which in the same period militarily unified China as a whole. Victorious by the late 1920s on several fronts, Chiang would remain at the helm of the GMD for the next half century, invoking Sun continuously as he did so.

One way that Chiang linked himself to Sun was to preside at his final burial near Nanjing. As early as 1925, a competition was held among architects to select the design for Sun's future mausoleum. The winning design combined Western and Chinese elements and construction was begun the following year. Between 1926 and 1929, the GMD government spent more than one million dollars—a vast sum at the time—to build Sun's giant mausoleum on Purple Mountain. The structures comprising the mausoleum required 80,000 square feet of marble and the route to the summit—where the sepulcher was located—entailed a climb up almost 400 steps. Inside the main building, the walls were covered with Sun's quotations while a giant GMD flag decorated the ceiling. To connect the entire mausoleum to the nearby city of Nanjing, the government constructed an eight-mile long, 140-foot wide memorial parkway. Sadly, peasants whose houses were confiscated to create the parkway received virtually no compensation for their losses and more than a hundred of them committed suicide in desperation.

The actual reburial in June 1929 was as lavish as one might imagine. First, a luxuriously appointed train transported Sun's remains 600 miles from Beijing to Nanjing. In line with the new image of Sun that the GMD government promoted, he was now attired in a Confucian scholar's gown rather than in the Western suit he had worn when he lay in state. As the train neared Nanjing, airplanes circled overhead and Chiang arrived with an armed escort to meet the funeral coach. The ceremony itself featured the participation of diplomats from dozens of countries and the attendance of thousands of ordinary citizens. Once the burial was complete, the propaganda value of having Sun interred on Purple Mountain was immense: GMD literature represented him as benevolently watching over the national government installed in the city of Nanjing below.

The Sun cult that took shape as the GMD consolidated its one-party rule over China in the early 1930s had a number of dimensions. However, its central component was the public reading of the Leader's Will every Monday morning. This took place at virtually every public location, be it a government office, an army barrack, a school, or even a factory. Everyone present would bow three times in front of a portrait of Sun, after which someone read out his will. The ceremony would conclude with three minutes of reverent silence and sometimes a patriotic song or lecture afterward.

Photo showing Sun Yatsen's bier being carried up the steps to his final resting place on Purple Mountain outside Nanjing in 1929. (*AP Wide World Photos*)

In 1940, Sun was elevated even further. From this time forward, instead of being known simply as leader—a title already reserved for him alone—he would be referred to as the "father of the nation [*guofu*]." Even today, GMD literature pertaining to Sun rarely utilizes his name, replacing it with "father of the nation" at every opportunity. In any case, by 1940 when the shift to father-of-the-nation took place, Sun's stature in China already soared high above that of any living human being.

It is worth reminding ourselves that the Sun Yatsen whom GMD leaders set on a high pedestal was not the person whose life and activities we have been following throughout this book. One contrast between Sun Yatsen and the image later erected in his place is especially revealing. Throughout his life, Sun strongly admired the Taiping rebels, whose mammoth effort to overthrow the Qing dynasty had been crushed around the time of his birth. Sun, like the rebels, opposed the Manchus and supported social equality. He especially identified with Hong Xiuquan, the rebellion's leader. When Chiang first took over the helm of the GMD in the late 1920s, he too spoke in praise of the Taiping Rebellion and Hong Xiuquan. Yet by the early 1930s, he had shifted: Instead of the rebels, it was the Qing government's successful effort to *suppress* the rebels that he extolled. Indeed, he reserved special praise for Zeng Guofan, the Confucian government official who took the lead in defeating the rebellion. Interestingly, Chiang made this shift without drawing any attention to the fact that he was now directly opposing Sun's view! Instead, he simply equated Sun with Confucius and by extension with loyal Confucian officials throughout Chinese history. There was a grain of truth to Chiang's approach, as Sun did indeed praise Chinese tradition. However, there was more to Sun's life and thought than Chiang was willing to admit. As we will see presently, other Chinese political movements that have invoked Sun share this tendency toward selective memory.

One figure who arrived at a new and jarring interpretation of Sun was his longtime follower Wang Jingwei. Wang had originally met Sun in Japan and had served as one of the main writers for the Revolutionary Alliance's organ, *The People's Journal.* Later, he served as a close advisor to Sun's Guangzhou governments and penned the Leader's Will that the GMD celebrated. As the GMD national government established itself after Chiang's Northern Expedition, Wang continued to play a central role. In the late 1930s, however, Japan invaded China, taking over most of its major cities, including Nanjing. As Wang became increasingly pessimistic that China could continue to hold out against Japan, he made the fateful decision to help the Japanese government establish a pro-Japanese state that would rule over central China. For the overwhelming majority of Chinese then and since, this was an act of treason.

The new state was proclaimed in Nanjing—the former GMD capital—in 1940. Wang, its highest official, continuously invoked Sun in order to justify his government's existence and actions. During World War II, Chiang Kaishek's government had been compelled to take refuge in the inland city of Chongqing. Wang alleged that Chiang's government was illegitimate and that instead his government was the true government of China. Indeed, he went further, claiming that his party was the true GMD, his flag was the true GMD flag, and his principles were the true Three People's Principles! He even organized the new Nanjing government with five separate branches in the manner recommended by Sun.

To rationalize his alliance with wartime Japan, Wang often referred to Sun's own friendship with Japan and especially to the pan-Asianist speech that Sun gave in Kobe several months before his death. Long before Wang defected during World War II, he had already stood out as the only figure among Sun's close followers who had inherited Sun's positive view of Japan. During his years of leadership in Nanjing, however, he pushed Sun's positive view a great distance beyond Sun himself, transforming it into a justification for Chinese subjection to Japan. Wang died in 1944; in the following year, the Allied powers of World War II defeated the Axis powers, including Japan. Wang's view that Sun would have supported an alliance with imperial Japan during World War II did not survive him.

Sun's Beatification, Post-1949

Sun Yatsen did not found the CCP as he did the GMD. Nevertheless, leaders of the CCP have long revered him as a major predecessor of the revolution by which they gained control over China in 1949. From the late 1920s through the 1970s, CCP respect for Sun centered around the notion of the "Three Great Policies," which for Chinese Communists nearly became a substitute for the Three People's Principles. Sun's Three Great Policies as depicted in CCP sources are (1) alliance with the Soviet Union, (2) collaboration with the CCP, and (3) support for the peasants' and workers' movements. By adopting these policies, Chinese Communists argued, Sun proved himself a close friend of the CCP and helped it to triumph under Mao Zedong's leadership a quarter of a century later.

The GMD does not deny that Sun advocated the policies listed in the "Three Great Policies." However, it disagrees strongly regarding their significance. While the CCP treated the policies as a late but permanent reorientation in Sun Yatsen's thinking, the GMD viewed them instead as temporary tactics aimed solely at obtaining assistance from the Soviet Union. It is impossible to resolve the issue definitively, as Sun did not live to see the challenges that the alliance would later face. However, it is clear that in the long term Sun wanted to see his own movement, rather than that of the CCP, rule over China. In that respect, the policies primarily reflect his eagerness for foreign aid. On the other hand, Sun's late verbal attacks on imperialism matched the CCP's outlook much more closely than they did that of the GMD under Chiang Kaishek. Consequently, while the CCP publicized those attacks, the GMD—eager to ally with the United States— quietly ignored them.

Sun has received great respect in the PRC since its establishment in 1949. There is at least one landmark—a park, a major avenue, or a square—named after Sun in virtually every city in China. This is especially striking because government policy generally forbids the naming of public locations after Communist leaders (e.g., there is no "Mao square" anywhere in the country). The result is that the name "Zhongshan" has an unusually high diffusion in Chinese urban areas, even exceeding that of the name "Washington" in American urban areas. In addition, a giant version of Sun's portrait is displayed annually in Tiananmen Square in Beijing for several weeks before and after October 1, the anniversary of the founding of the PRC. These actions and others—the renovation of buildings associated with his life, the production of movies glorifying his deeds, and so on—maintain Sun's name and visage in the consciousness of tens of millions of ordinary Chinese.

One surprising sign of Sun Yatsen's impact, at least during the early years of Communist rule, was sartorial. Photos of Chinese street scenes during the 1950s through 1970s typically show citizens wearing dark jackets that were buttoned to the collar. Westerners referred to the jackets as "Mao jackets," after Mao Zedong, who wore one and promoted them as the uniform of his people. In Chinese, however, they are called "Zhongshan zhuan," that is, Sun Yatsen outfits. Late in his career, Sun had commissioned a tailor to create a jacket that could serve as a nationalistic alternative to both traditional Chinese dress and the Western business suit. The jacket that the tailor devised, based primarily on military outfits, became Sun's visual trademark in his final years. Mao, in turn, modified the design of the jacket and issued it to citizens for everyday use while acknowledging its link with Sun through the "Zhongshan" name that his government employed for it.

In sum, Sun by no means disappeared under the Communists, who extolled his Three Great Policies, splashed his name liberally across urban settings, enforced his substitute for traditional Chinese dress, and bestowed numerous honors on his last wife, Soong Qingling. While the Communist government does not usually refer to Sun as the "father of the nation" in the manner of the GMD, it has nevertheless found a variety of ways to present him as a progenitor of modern China.

Despite all of the glorification of Sun Yatsen, during Mao's lifetime there was usually a hint of condescension in Chinese Communist praise for him. Sun, the party line suggested, was indeed antifeudal and anti-imperialist, but he was not *as* antifeudal and anti-imperialist as the CCP would later be. Mao asserted as much when he cautioned people in Communist China not to be overly critical of the

Sun Yatsen wearing his trademark jacket
in front of his Shanghai residence in 1924.
(*Courtesy of the Library of Congress*)

mistakes of early twentieth-century revolutionaries like Sun. After Mao died in 1976, however, the official CCP view began to lose its condescension. At the end of the 1970s, moderate Communists led by Deng Xiaoping sought to move away from the radicalism of the Mao era and toward technological modernization through large-scale foreign investment. As part of this, Deng began to promote "socialism with Chinese characteristics," that is, a (very) roughly equal distribution of China's wealth once it has first been generated by capitalist means. This closely matched Sun's recommendation in *The International Development of China*, as did the sheer scale of the public works projects that Deng and others advocated. Reflecting these objectives, the government began to say less about Sun's Three Great Policies and much more about his support for a state-directed, foreign-assisted effort to modernize China's economy.

Simultaneous with this shift, Sun became useful to the leaders of the PRC in still another way. Ever since the CCP victory in 1949, two distinct governments claimed that they were the legitimate government over China as a whole. One of these governments was the Communist government of the PRC, which did in fact control the entire Chinese mainland. The other government was the GMD-led government of the Republic of China on Taiwan. Throughout the era of Mao's rule, these two governments aggressively condemned each other. However, after both Mao and Chiang died in the mid-1970s, the PRC took a new tack: Instead of—or rather, in addition to—threatening Taiwan militarily, it began diplomatic efforts aimed at attracting Taiwan to reunify with the PRC through a peaceful political process. If reunification took place, Taiwan would have to permit the PRC to control its foreign policy (the GMD could continue to handle the island's domestic affairs). In exchange, however, Taiwan would no longer have to arm itself against possible invasion from the mainland. GMD leaders displayed a guarded interest in this offer and talks began between the two sides. In these talks, each side regularly invoked Sun Yatsen's Three People's Principles as a possible basis for reunification: After all, both claimed to honor Sun's commitments to nationalism, democracy, and people's livelihood. The PRC's efforts to employ Sun as a bridge to Taiwan reached a climax in 2005 when Lien Chan, then the chair of the GMD, visited Sun's mausoleum in Nanjing on an elaborate official visit and solemnly paid his respects alongside CCP leaders. If reunification between the PRC and Taiwan ever does occur, it is safe to assume that Sun's name and memory will figure prominently at every stage of the process.

Sun as Nationalistic Dreamer

Sun Yatsen lived and worked during an era in which the power of the West—Europe and its offshoots, the United States and Russia—was extending its reach across virtually the entire earth. This process of expansion created frequent and unequal cultural encounters between Westerners and people of other nationalities. According to political scientist Mary Matossian, one effect of these encounters wherever they occurred was to produce an indigenous intelligentsia with special characteristics: an acceptance of a modern scientific outlook, a sense of their own nation's vulnerability, and a fierce desire to see their nation industrialize and modernize to regain its power. All of these characteristics appear in Sun Yatsen and his closest followers.

To bring about the industrialization and modernization that indigenous intellectuals in China and elsewhere prized, state power was regarded as vital. Whatever furthered the power of the state was regarded positively, while whatever harmed it was regarded negatively. We see this even in how Sun and others responded to socialism: They celebrated it insofar as it increased government control over the economy, while they feared it in the Marxist form that pitted social classes within the nation against each other. Overall, what modern nationalists outside the West sought to create was a paternalistic state that protected its citizens from foreign domination and gross economic exploitation while demanding a high degree of loyalty from those citizens in return. Their favorite method of bringing this vision to fruition was through the creation of a political party that would gain power and put its nationalistic program into effect.

Sun created a number of political organizations in his lifetime—the Revive China Society, the Revolutionary Alliance, and so forth—but the one that lasted was the Guomindang. He had taken little interest in the party in 1912, when its purpose was merely to become the majority party in parliament. He returned to it in 1919, however, following the failure of his first Guangzhou government, and nurtured it for the last six years of his life. In practice, this party had little influence until Soviet advisor Mikhail Borodin taught Sun how to reorganize it along

Soviet lines. The resulting party was highly centralized, yet flexible enough to exploit a variety of events and organizations for its own purposes. Following Sun's death, it managed either to overpower or to outmaneuver its warlord competitors and reunify China—loosely. Some 20 years and two horrific wars later, a still more supple version of the Soviet model—the Chinese Communist Party—brought about a more secure and sometimes stifling reunification that has lasted, with modifications, to the present day.

For most Chinese, Sun represents less the final results of reunification—the prosaic reality of a government that aims to please the constituencies vital to its preservation—than an early expression of the *desire* for such reunification and especially for the peace, national power, and individual prosperity it could yield. Like nationalists in other lands, Sun was a dreamer who embodied his dreams in institutions. All too often, these institutions have claimed that whatever they decide to do is by definition an expression of those dreams. Counterbalancing this, succeeding generations may always recall the words of the dreamer—nationalism, democracy, and people's livelihood—to hold the institutions accountable for any nightmarish departures. In this respect, seeking a newer China—and world—ceases to be the story of one individual, becoming instead a never-ending process.

Study Questions

The following 15 study questions typically draw on material from more than one chapter in the text. In addition, several questions link Sun Yatsen and his Chinese context with larger issues in modern world history. As the questions are interpretative, there is a degree of leeway in how different individuals may respond to them.

1. Why is it significant that Sun Yatsen was born and raised in southern China as opposed to another part of the country? What were the advantages and disadvantages for him of hailing from that region? How did his southern origins affect his later revolutionary strategy?

2. How did Sun Yatsen view the Taiping Rebellion? Under what circumstances did he first learn about it? How did its example help shape his later thought and activity as an anti-Qing revolutionary?

3. Based on Li Hongzhang's participation in the Self-Strengthening Movement, what would you say his solution was to the challenge that Western military power presented to late Qing China? How did Sun Yatsen view Li before he presented him with his 1894 letter of advice? How did his attitude change later?

4. The kidnapping of Sun Yatsen by the Chinese Legation in London played a major role in his subsequent career as an anti-Qing revolutionary. In what ways did the event affect the way Chinese people viewed him, the way Westerners viewed him, and the way he viewed himself, respectively? How might his revolutionary career have proceeded differently had he not experienced the kidnapping in London?

5. In later years, Sun Yatsen called ethnic Chinese living overseas the "mother of the revolution." What did he mean by that? What difficulties did Sun face in trying to appeal to this widely scattered group of people? What techniques did he employ to overcome these difficulties and expand his influence among them?

6. What did Sun Yatsen's Revolutionary Alliance achieve in China and abroad? Who opposed the Alliance and what actions did they take to express their

opposition? What tensions within the Alliance threatened its existence and how did the organization try to handle them? What happened to the Alliance after the 1911 revolution?

7. Many Chinese respect Sun Yatsen for his Three People's Principles. What conflicting values—indigenous and/or foreign—do the principles attempt to synthesize together? Discuss with reference to each of the principles. In your opinion, how successful was Sun's effort to blend together the values he respected?

8. In what respects did Sun Yatsen help bring about the 1911 revolution in China? In what respects was he essentially irrelevant to its unfolding? In your view, what revolution elsewhere in the world in modern times most closely resembled this one? What were the major points of resemblance?

9. What made Yuan Shikai so influential during the final years of the Qing dynasty? Why did the revolutionaries of 1911 and the parliament members of 1912 feel that they needed to compromise with him? What regimes elsewhere in the world in modern times have depended on Western financial assistance in the manner of Yuan's government? Focusing on two examples of your choice, what was the *quid pro quo* in each case between Western nations and the non-Western regime that received their aid?

10. Sun Yatsen's entire revolutionary career was affected by his close political and emotional ties with influential Japanese. How did Sun try to capitalize on these ties as he fought against the Qing dynasty, Yuan Shikai, and warlordism, respectively? What types of assistance, if any, was Sun able to receive as a result of his Japanese connections?

11. Sun's revolutionary career intersected with Chinese student activism on two important occasions: in 1905, among Chinese students living in Japan and in 1919, among Chinese students living in coastal Chinese cities. How were the aims and outlooks of the students in these two cases similar? How were they different? How did Sun's responses to the two movements contrast?

12. How did Chinese warlordism shape the last decade of Sun Yatsen's life? What was Sun's approach to eliminating warlordism from Chinese society? At which points in time did his own behavior resemble that of the warlords? Name one other country in modern times that has been afflicted by warlordism and describe how—if at all—its situation was resolved in favor of a greater centralization of power.

13. Between 1923 and 1927, the GMD and the Soviet Union were politically allied. Focusing on the 1923–1925 period, what advantages did the alliance provide to each side? What dissatisfactions did each side experience vis-à-vis its partner? What new circumstance would eventually cause the termination of the alliance in 1927?

14. After the life-span of a famous person or movement has reached its end, individuals and groups typically begin to recall, selectively, what the person or movement had been like. Taken together, historians call the history of these acts of recollection a "reception history." Name and discuss three major events in the political history of China since Sun's death in 1925 that have strongly affected the reception history of his life and thought. In your opinion, which of the events you selected had the greatest impact on Chinese people's images of Sun? Why?

15. Sun Yatsen was one of a number of nationalist leaders in various parts of the world in the late nineteenth and early twentieth centuries. Which nationalist leader from that historical era would you compare to Sun Yatsen? What are the most prominent similarities between Sun and the leader you have selected? What are several important differences between the two leaders?

Chronology

1644	The Qing dynasty begins
1839–1841	The Opium War between Great Britain and China takes place and ends with a victory for Great Britain
1842	The Treaty of Nanjing, the first in a series of "unequal treaties," is signed between Great Britain and China
1851–1864	The Taiping Rebellion takes place
1866	Sun Yatsen is born in the village of Cuiheng in Guangdong province
1879	Sun travels to Hawaii to join his brother Sun Mei, entering Iolani School after he arrives
1883	Sun is baptized at the American Congregational Mission Church in Hong Kong
1884	Sun marries his first wife, Lu Muzhen
1884–1885	The Sino-French War, fought between China and France regarding control over Annam, is won by France
1886	Sun begins to study medicine at the Canton Medical School in Guangzhou
1887	Sun transfers to the College of Medicine for Chinese in Hong Kong
1892	Sun graduates from the College of Medicine for Chinese and establishes a clinic in Macao
1894	Sun abandons medical practice, petitions Qing official Li Hongzhang, and creates the Revive China Society in Honolulu
1894–1895	The Sino-Japanese War, fought between China and Japan over influence in Korea, leads to a Japanese victory and the Treaty of Shimonoseki
1895	Sun organizes a failed uprising in Guangzhou against the Qing government, escaping afterward to Japan
1896	Sun, in exile, is kidnapped by the Qing government in the Chinese Legation in London
1897	Sun publishes *Kidnapped in London* and meets Miyazaki Tôten in Japan

1898	The Hundred Days of Reform takes place, prompting the Empress Dowager Cixi to reassert her power within the Qing government
1899	Reformist leader Kang Youwei founds the Emperor Protection Society in Canada
1900	Sun organizes the failed Huizhou Uprising, timed to coincide with the Boxer Uprising of the same year
1901	The Qing dynasty begins its New Policies, intended to recast the dynasty as a modern government
1902–1903	Reformer Liang Qichao publishes the *New Citizen Review* in Japan
1904–1905	The Russo-Japanese War, fought between Russia and Japan over the issue of control over Korea, ends in a Japanese victory
1905	Sun and others establish the Revolutionary Alliance in Tokyo, Japan
1906–1908	Sun organizes a series of failed uprisings in southern China with tacit French Indochinese cooperation
1907	Sun is expelled from Japan
1908	The Empress Dowager Cixi and Emperor Guangxu die, resulting in the ascension of Puyi, a child emperor
1911	A failed uprising in Guangzhou is followed seven months later, on October 10, by the Wuchang Uprising that causes the steady collapse of the Qing dynasty and prompts Sun's return to China
1912	Sun becomes Provisional President of the Republic of China, Yuan Shikai succeeds him, and the Revolutionary Alliance is reorganized as the GMD
1913	Song Jiaoren, de facto leader of the GMD, is assassinated, leading Sun to attempt a failed military campaign against President Yuan Shikai
1914	Yuan Shikai dissolves parliament and promulgates a new constitution; Sun marries his final wife, Soong Qingling, in Tokyo
1914–1918	World War I rages, primarily in Europe
1915	Yuan attempts to restore the Chinese monarchy with himself as emperor of a new dynasty
1916	Yuan is compelled to abandon his monarchical plans and dies in midyear
1916–1927	Period of pervasive warlordism in China
1917	Sun opposes the Beijing government's decision to enter World War I on the Allied side, establishing his first Guangzhou government in protest
1918–1920	Following the failure of the first Guangzhou government, Sun spends two years in Shanghai writing *Memoirs of a Chinese Revolutionary* and *The International Development of China*

1919	The May Fourth Incident, a response to the terms of the proposed Versailles Treaty, sparks an upsurge in Chinese student nationalism
1920	Sun creates his second Guangzhou government
1922	Chen Jiongming, a southern warlord, drives Sun out of Guangzhou, ending his second Guangzhou government
1923	Sun and Soviet representative Adolf Joffe issue a joint statement, Comintern agent Mikhail Borodin arrives in Guangzhou, and Sun appoints Chiang Kaishek as superintendent of the Huangpu Military Academy
1924	Sun presides over the First National Congress of the Guomindang and delivers his lectures on the Three People's Principles; late in the year, he travels to Beijing to confer with major warlords, falling ill along the way
1925	Sun dies of cancer in Beijing, China, at age 58
1926	Following an internal power struggle, Chiang Kaishek takes control of the GMD
1926–1928	Chiang Kaishek leads a successful Northern Expedition to unify China, purging the GMD of Communists along the way
1927	Chiang Kaishek marries Soong Meiling, sister of Sun's final wife
1929	Sun's body is transported to Nanjing and ceremoniously reburied in a massive hillside mausoleum
1937	The Japanese government launches a full-scale attack on the eastern seaboard of China and occupies most of China's major cities
1940	Wang Jingwei sets up a pro-Japanese government in Nanjing
1943	The last of the "unequal treaties" between China and powerful Western nations are finally abrogated
1945	World War II ends with victory for the Allied powers, including the Republic of China
1946–1949	A civil war rages between the GMD led by Chiang Kaishek and the CCP led by Mao Zedong
1949	The CCP wins the civil war and establishes the PRC, causing GMD forces to flee to the island of Taiwan and continue the Republic of China there
1975	Chiang Kaishek dies
1976	Mao Zedong dies, opening the door in the PRC for reformist Communists who favor plans similar to Sun's for economic development
1981	Sun's final wife, Soong Qingling, dies in Beijing at age 88

Glossary

General Notes

The pronunciation guides that I provide below for Chinese terms are approximate and do not include tones, an essential part of correct Chinese pronunciation.

Note: The vowel sound that I spell as "**ah**" (e.g., "kahng") in the guides is the sound of "o" in "on" or "top," while the vowel sound I spell as "**uh**" (e.g., "tsuh") is the sound of "u" in "luck."

For alphabetical listing purposes, Western names are presented with the family name first. As Chinese and Japanese names already begin with the family name, they are presented in the same order as in the main text.

In certain cases, I provide the original Chinese terms for items given solely in English in the main text. This is to assist readers who wish to delve further into the English-language academic literature on Sun Yatsen, which sometimes employs these terms. With the same intention, I occasionally provide alternate spellings for common Chinese terms.

Beijing (Bay-JING)   The capital of China during most of Sun's lifetime and today. The respective governments of the Manchus, Yuan Shikai, and various northern warlord alliances all ruled from Beijing, rendering it the ultimate target for Sun Yatsen's efforts to unify China under his rule. Called "Peking" (or occasionally "Peiping") in older English literature.

Borodin, Mikhail (Baw-ruh-DEEN)   An agent for the Communist International (Comintern). Borodin represented the Soviet Union in its efforts to aid and reorganize the GMD during 1923–1927.

Boxer Uprising   A traditional-style rebellion against Western imperialism in China. The instigators, called Boxers because of certain exercises they performed that allegedly gave them magical powers, took a number of Westerners hostage in Beijing in 1900. This sparked a successful multinational effort to rescue the hostages and humiliate the Qing government for having sided with the rebels.

Cantlie, James   A Scottish missionary and doctor who taught Sun Yatsen at the College of Medicine for Chinese in Hong Kong. Cantlie became Sun's greatest

British admirer, providing him indispensable assistance during the kidnapping incident in London in 1896 and promoting his causes in subsequent decades.

CCP   Abbreviation for Chinese Communist Party.

Chen Jiongming (CHEN Jyawng-MING)   A warlord and statesman during the late 1910s and early 1920s in Guangdong province in southern China. Originally a follower of Sun Yatsen, he violently broke with Sun during the latter's second Guangzhou government, leading to that government's fall in 1922. Chen's federalism, or support for a loose political association of China's provinces, sharply contrasted with the ideologies of both the GMD and the CCP.

Chinese Communist Party   A political party established with Soviet assistance in 1921. The party grew in size through its 1923–1927 alliance with the GMD, and later, through its resistance to Japan's invasion of China in World War II. It achieved control over China as a whole in 1949 and remains in power there today.

Chiang Kaishek (Jee-AHNG Kai-SHEK)   Leader of the GMD from 1926 until his death in Taiwan in 1975. Chiang was known for his vehement opposition to the CCP and his advocacy of Confucian social morality. "Chiang Kaishek" is the Cantonese rendering of his name; speakers of standard Chinese know him as Jiang Jieshi.

Cixi, Empress Dowager (Tsuh-SHEE)   A concubine of a mid-nineteenth century Qing emperor, she subsequently exerted vast and primarily conservative influence over Chinese politics during the reigns of her son Tongzhi (1861–1875) and her nephew Guangxu (1875–1908).

Comintern   "Communist International," an organization created by the Soviet Union in 1919 to spread Communist revolution to countries around the world. Through most of the 1920s, it concentrated its efforts on fomenting revolution in colonized and semicolonized nations like China.

Cuiheng (Tsway-HUNG)   The village in Guangdong province where Sun Yatsen was born in 1866. Cuiheng has become a prominent tourist destination owing to its association with Sun.

Emperor Protection Society   An organization established by noted reformist Kang Youwei in Canada in 1899. The organization's aim was to oppose the Empress Dowager Cixi while seeking restoration of the reform-minded Emperor Guangxu to effective political power. Called *Baohuanghui* in Chinese.

Extraterritoriality   The principle, asserted in the "unequal treaties" between powerful Western nations and China, that Western residents in China who commit crimes should be tried by the laws of their home countries rather than those of China. Meanwhile, Chinese nationals visiting Western countries would still be subject to the laws of those countries rather than Chinese laws.

George, Henry   A social reformer in the late nineteenth-century United States. George advocated in his *Progress and Poverty* that the government appropriate as its "single tax" all increases in land prices caused by speculation and eliminate all other taxes. This proposal attracted support from Sun Yatsen and others abroad.

GMD   Abbreviation for Guomindang.

Guangxu, Emperor (GWAHNG-shoo)   Nephew of the Empress Dowager Cixi. Guangxu officially reigned during 1875–1908 but only attempted to rule during the short-lived Hundred Days of Reform of 1898, after which Cixi kept him under effectual house arrest.

Guangzhou (Guahng-JOE)   The capital of Guangdong province and the largest port city in southern China. In early struggles against the Manchus and later ones against the warlords, Sun attempted to seize Guangzhou and use it as his base for conquering China as a whole. Older English literature refers to the city as Canton.

Guomindang (Gwo-min-DAHNG)   Meaning "Nationalist Party" in Chinese, the Guomindang, founded by Sun Yatsen, became a conservative party after his death. It ruled virtually all of China from 1928 until 1949, when the Chinese Communist Party forced it to evacuate the Chinese mainland and reestablish itself on the island of Taiwan. Called Kuomintang or KMT in older sources.

Hong Kong (HAWNG KAWNG)   During Sun's lifetime, a British colonial possession in southeast China that included a rocky island with a deepwater harbor and territories adjoining the island on the Chinese mainland. Sun spent five years (1887–1892) in Hong Kong as a medical student and later established important branches of his anti-Qing revolutionary organizations there.

Huang Xing (Hwahng SHING)   A cofounder of the Revolutionary Alliance. Huang led uprisings against the Qing dynasty in southern provinces, served in Sun's Nanjing provisional government, and, later, broke with Sun over the latter's reorganization of the GMD. He died in 1916 after reconciling with Sun.

Huangpu Military Academy (HWAHNG-poo)   Formally founded in Guangzhou in 1924 with massive Soviet aid and headed by Chiang Kaishek, the academy trained a generation of GMD (and some CCP) generals who led forces in the Northern Expedition, World War II, and the Chinese Civil War. Called Whampoa in older English literature.

Huizhou Uprising (Hway-JOE)   A Revive China Society-coordinated uprising of secret society forces in Guangdong in late 1900 that sought to capitalize on the Qing dynasty's difficulties in the wake of the Boxer Uprising. Its initial success demonstrated the existence of popular support for anti-Qing military efforts. Spelled Waichow in an earlier type of transliteration called Wade-Giles.

Hundred Days of Reform   A failed attempt on the part of Emperor Guangxu and reformist advisors during the summer of 1898 to reorganize the Qing dynasty extensively along the lines of Meiji Japan. The immediate objective was to strengthen China in the wake of Western nations' scramble for concessions along China's seacoast.

Kang Youwei (KAHNG Yo-WAY)   A late nineteenth- and early twentieth-century Confucian scholar who sought to reinterpret Confucius in such a way as to justify extensive modernization in China while shutting the door to outright termination of the monarchy. Kang created the Emperor Protection Society to spread his views.

Lenin, Vladimir The leading instigator of the Russian Revolution (1917) and premier of the Soviet Union until his death in 1924. Under Lenin's rule, the Soviet Union aimed to spread Communism throughout the world and especially to colonized and semicolonized nations like China.

Li Hongzhang (Lee Hawng-JAHNG) Holder of various posts in the Qing government. Li was the most influential official in late nineteenth-century China, spearheading the effort to build up China militarily and industrially even as he sought to maintain primarily friendly relations with powerful Western nations. Li died in 1901 after negotiating the humiliating Boxer Protocols that followed the failure of the Boxer Uprising.

Liang Qichao (Lee-AHNG Chee-CHOW) A late nineteenth- and early twentieth-century reformist who began as a Confucianist and became increasingly enamored with modern Western thought. Liang promoted his views—especially that of creating political strength through social unity—in stylish essays that influenced generations of nationalistic Chinese.

Lu Haodong (LOO How-DAWNG) A childhood friend of Sun Yatsen. Lu accompanied Sun on his trip to visit Li Hongzhang in Tianjin and helped Sun plan the 1895 Guangzhou Uprising. His participation in the uprising led to his arrest and execution in the same year.

Lu Muzhen (LOO Moo-JUHN) Sun Yatsen's first wife. Sun married her in 1884 and together they had three children—a son and two daughters. Sun amicably parted with Lu to marry Soong Qingling in 1915.

Manchus A nomadic ethnic group hailing from Manchuria, a large arid region northeast of the Great Wall. The Manchus ruled over China during the Qing dynasty (1644–1912).

Mao Zedong (MAO Tsuh-DAWNG) The overall leader of the CCP (1935–1976) and the PRC (1949–1976), Mao instigated massive and often violent efforts to modernize China while bringing it in line with his purist, radical version of Communism.

May Fourth Movement A movement primarily among Chinese students and intellectuals during the late 1910s and early 1920s. It sought to strengthen China by eliminating Chinese tradition and embracing modern science and democracy. Its name derives from a large patriotic demonstration held in Beijing on May 4, 1919.

Meiji Restoration (MAY-jee) The "restoration" of the Japanese emperor to a position of official power in 1868 after centuries of warrior rule. The underlying aim was to unify and modernize Japan in order to prevent powerful Western nations from colonizing the country. The restoration was followed by the 44-year-long reign of Emperor Meiji.

Miyazaki Tôten (MEE-yuh-zah-kee TOE-ten) Sun Yatsen's closest Japanese friend and a source of contacts for Sun with powerful Japanese officials, including future premier Inukai Tsuyoshi. Also called Miyazaki Torazô.

New Policies The promodernization policies in such fields as education, government structure, and military organization that the Qing government promoted in the wake of the disastrous Boxer Uprising of 1900. While the government fully committed itself to the policies, they had the ironic effect of empowering provincial elites that eventually supported the anti-Qing revolution in 1911.

Northern Expedition   Originating in a strategy promoted by Sun Yatsen, this massive military campaign northward from Guangzhou to Beijing (1926–1928) led to the conquest of numerous warlord armies and provided the basis for a unified Republic of China under GMD rule.

Opium War   A war waged between Great Britain and China during 1839–1841 over British companies' importation of opium into China. The war ended with a victory for Great Britain, which in a series of treaties demanded and received an indemnity, the island of Hong Kong, extraterritorial privileges in designated coastal ports, and the right to continue to export opium to China.

People's Journal   The official newspaper for the Revolutionary Alliance between 1905 and 1908. Essays in the newspaper by skilled writers like Zhang Binglin and Wang Jingwei argued strongly in favor of overthrowing the Manchu monarchy as a step toward China's modernization. Called *Minbao* in Chinese.

People's Livelihood   The most controversial of Sun Yatsen's Three People's Principles, people's livelihood refers to the provision of the daily necessities of life to the people of China through a prosperous economy and a degree of wealth redistribution. Called *minsheng* in Chinese.

People's Republic of China   The official name of China expect for Taiwan and, for several decades, Hong Kong and Macao since 1949, when the CCP first took control by defeating the GMD nationwide. Sometimes referred to as mainland China.

PRC   Abbreviation for People's Republic of China.

Qing Dynasty (CHING)   The last dynasty in Chinese history. The Qing (lit. "pure") period lasted from 1644 to 1912 and featured the rule of ethnic Manchus, nomads from the northeast of the Great Wall, over a far larger Chinese population. Spelled "Ch'ing" in many older sources.

Republic of China   The government that Sun Yatsen established in 1912. Under GMD leadership, it ruled over virtually all of China from 1928 to 1949. When the GMD escaped to the island of Taiwan in 1949, it reestablished the Republic of China there and permitted it to evolve over time into a multiparty state. Sometimes abbreviated as ROC.

Revive China Society   The organization that Sun Yatsen created in Honolulu, Hawaii, in 1895 among Chinese immigrant supporters to promote the overthrow of the Qing dynasty through a southern-based rebellion. Called *Xingzhonghui* in Chinese.

Revolutionary Alliance   The umbrella organization that Sun Yatsen and others founded in Tokyo, Japan, in 1905 to coordinate efforts to overthrow the Qing dynasty. Called *Tongmenghui* in Chinese and translated by some authors as United League.

Russo-Japanese War   A war waged on both land and sea between Russia and Japan in 1904–1905 regarding control over Korea. The war ended with victory for Japan, enabling Japan to annex Korea outright in 1910.

Scramble for Concessions   An intense competition among powerful Western nations in 1897–1898 for spheres of influence along China's eastern seaboard.

Second Revolution   A military rebellion that Sun Yatsen promoted in 1913 against the increasingly dictatorial rule of Yuan Shikai. Only a few provinces joined and it rapidly collapsed.

Secret Society   The name used in English for a type of organization in Qing-dynasty China that promoted mutual aid among its often impoverished members. A number of secret societies called for the restoration of the preceding Ming dynasty, rendering them attractive to Sun Yatsen.

Self-Strengthening Movement   A movement among some late nineteenth-century Qing dynasty officials to strengthen China militarily and to a limited degree industrially. The movement's aim was to fend off any deeper political or cultural influence from Western nations.

Sino-French War   A war waged between China and France in 1884–1885 regarding control over Annam (part of present-day Vietnam). The war ended with victory for France, enabling it to establish Indochina as a colony comprised of Annam and neighboring territories.

Sino-Japanese War   A war waged on both land and sea between China and Japan in 1894–1895 regarding influence over Korea. The war ended with victory for Japan, enabling it to demand and receive the island of Taiwan, extraterritorial rights in designated Chinese port cities, and a large indemnity.

Song Jiaoren (SAWNG Jee-ow-REN)   A creator of the GMD and the leader of that party to victory in legislative elections in 1912–1913. Song was assassinated, probably by Yuan Shikai's agents, in early 1913.

Soong, Charlie (SAWNG)   Father of the famous Soong sisters, including Soong Qingling. During the early twentieth century, Charlie Soong was a self-made wealthy businessman in Shanghai and a central figure within China's Christian community.

Soong Qingling (SAWNG Ching-LING)   Sun Yatsen's final wife. Qingling enjoyed a Western-style romantic marriage with Sun and outlived him by over 50 years to become an outspoken supporter of the CCP. Alternate spellings include, among others, Song Qingling and Soong Ching Ling.

Spheres of Influence   In China, regions (usually coastal) technically under the control of the Chinese government. Within each such region, an imperial power would possess extensive rights to build railroads and extract timber and mineral resources. Spheres of influence were established during the 1897–1898 scramble for concessions and remained in existence until their abolition by common agreement at the Washington Conference of 1921–1922.

Sun Fo (Sawn FO)   Sun Yatsen's only son and the mayor of Guangzhou during Sun's second and third Guangzhou governments. Also known as Sun Ke.

Sun Mei (Sawn MAY)   Sun Yatsen's older brother. Sun Mei preceded his brother to Hawaii, succeeded in business there, and assisted Sun Yatsen and his family financially in the later 1890s and early 1900s.

Taiping Rebellion   The bloodiest war in world history up to its time. Many southern Chinese rebelled against the Qing dynasty (1851–1864) and attempted, at horrific human cost, to replace it with a Christian-influenced Taiping (lit. "heavenly peace") regime.

Taiwan   A large island off the southeast coast of China. Japan received the island as a colony as part of the spoils of the Sino-Japanese War. In 1949, it became the site of the Republic of China.

Three People's Principles   Democracy, Nationalism, and People's Livelihood, the three bases on which Sun Yatsen sought to establish a strong, modern China. Called *sanminzhuyi* in Chinese.

Treaty of Nanjing (Nan-JING)   A treaty signed in 1842 between the governments of Great Britain and China at the conclusion of the Opium War. The provisions of the treaty gave Great Britain an indemnity, the island of Hong Kong, and the right to trade at several previously closed ports, including Shanghai. Some sources refer to the treaty as the Treaty of Nanking.

Treaty of Shimonoseki (Shee-mo-no-SEH-kee)   A treaty signed in 1895 between the governments of China and Japan at the conclusion of the Sino-Japanese War. The provisions of the treaty gave Japan the island of Taiwan, extraterritorial rights in designated Chinese port cities, and a large indemnity.

"Unequal Treaties"   A series of treaties that Qing China signed with powerful Western nations (mainly 1840s) and Japan (1895) that gave those nations special privileges in China, including the right of extraterritoriality in designated port cities. The last unequal provisions of these treaties were abrogated in 1943.

Versailles Conference (Ver-SAI)   A conference held in Versailles, France, in 1919 among the victorious Allies of World War I to resolve postwar land issues in Europe and elsewhere. Its leading figures unintentionally heightened Chinese nationalism by permitting Japan to retain its privileges in China's Shandong peninsula, captured from Germany during the war.

Wang Jingwei (WAHNG Jing-WAY)   One of the leading figures in Sun Yatsen's Guangzhou governments and in the GMD subsequently. In 1940, he decided to cooperate with the invading Japanese military, agreeing to lead a puppet state headquartered in Nanjing. For this, most Chinese today regard him as a traitor to China.

Washington Conference   A conference sponsored by the United States and held among major Pacific naval powers (1921–1922). Conferees agreed to respect China's territorial sovereignty and recognized the warlord-led Beijing government as the legitimate government over China.

Wuchang Uprising (Woo-CHAHNG)   Occurring on October 10 ("Double Ten"), 1911, this uprising of government troops in Wuchang against the Qing dynasty directly brought about the latter's fall the following year.

Yuan Shikai (Yoo-AHN Shee-KAI)   Leader of the Qing dynasty's modernized forces and second president of the Republic of China. Ignoring restrictions on his power as president, he used his position to establish himself as a military strongman, leading Sun to organize a failed attempt to overthrow him. Following Yuan's death in 1916, his highest ranking followers set themselves up as regional warlords.

Zheng Shiliang (JAWNG Shuh-lee-AHNG)   A Christian friend of Sun Yatsen during the 1890s. Zheng introduced Sun to the Triad secret society—and secret societies generally—as a major source of anti-Manchu military muscle.

A Note on the Sources

As the reputed "father" of modern China, Sun Yatsen has attracted a very great amount of both scholarly and acclamatory attention. This literature in both Western and non-Western languages has been tentatively catalogued in Sidney H. Chang and Leonard H. D. Gordon, eds., *Bibliography of Sun Yat-sen in China's Republican Revolution*, 2nd ed. (Lanham, MD: University Press of America, 1998). I have relied almost exclusively on English-language sources for this biography. In my remarks below, I indicate which sources I utilized in the course of writing specific chapters of the book.

To begin with, however, I will provide a general description of a few works that were particularly central to my understanding of Sun. Sun himself wrote several books, all of which I read in English translation. His earliest book was *Kidnapped in London* (London: China Society, 1969), originally written in English and ghost-written at least in part by James Cantlie. The second book, *Memoirs of a Chinese Revolutionary: A Programme of National Reconstruction for China* (New York: Ams Press, 1970), displays Sun's frame of mind at the end of the 1910s and includes a chapter-long autobiographical sketch. The third book, *The International Development of China* (Taipei: China Cultural Service, 1953), was, like the second one, written during Sun's stay in Shanghai between 1918 and 1920. It lays out a very detailed plan for Chinese industrial development and contains certain passages that appear repeatedly in biographies of Sun.

Finally, there is Sun's most famous book among generations of Chinese, *San Min Chu I: The Three Principles of the People* (Taipei: Government Information Office, 1990). This work comprises 16 speeches that Sun gave in 1924 outlining his Three People's Principles, along with 2 speeches Chiang Kaishek gave later regarding the third principle, people's livelihood. Regrettably, the translation is actually an abridgement of the Chinese original, with some of Sun's more peculiar ideas quietly omitted from the text (the work's abridged status is not indicated in its front or back matter). Despite this defect, the work is an indispensable summation of Sun's thinking with regard to the future of his country. In addition to these books, there are also several collections of Sun's speeches and essays that I reference below in discussions of specific chapters.

The two Sun biographers who have most greatly influenced my thinking on Sun's life and its significance are Harold Z. Schiffrin and Marie-Claire Bergère.

Schiffrin's classic work is *Sun Yat-sen and the Origins of the Chinese Revolution* (Berkeley: University of California Press, 1970; hereafter, *Origins*). Schiffrin's approach is to avoid presenting Sun as either a hero or a villain, treating him instead as a courageous but egotistical political operator who sought to strengthen China through modernization. While this work takes the story of Sun's life only as far as 1905, a later and shorter biography by Schiffrin, *Sun Yat-sen: Reluctant Revolutionary* (Boston: Little Brown, 1980), provides birth-to-death coverage.

Marie-Claire Bergère is the author of *Sun Yat-sen* (Stanford University Press, 1980), an ambitious work that places Sun extensively into his national and international environment. Bergère's foremost themes, overlapping with Schiffrin's, are Sun's cultural marginality, his skill at communicating with diverse audiences, and his ability to project himself into the future. There are also several other important biographers of Sun, whose biographies I reference below in my discussions of specific chapters.

Preface

The historian who claims that Sun "tried to go way beyond his" potential is Harold Z. Schiffrin in his *Sun Yat-sen*, p. 4. The historian whom I quote as having characterized Sun Yatsen as the "traveling salesman of the [Chinese] revolution" is Marie-Claire Bergère in her *Sun Yat-sen*, p. 139. The quotation from Mark Twain regarding the nineteenth century appears in Paul Fatout, ed., *Mark Twain Speaking* (Iowa City: University of Iowa Press, 1976), p. 244. In my discussion of historiographical issues, the works that exemplify the "new approach" to the Guomindang in the 1920s are John Fitzgerald, *Awakening China: Politics, Culture, and Class in the Nationalist Revolution* (Stanford, CA: Stanford University Press, 1996), Michael Tsin, *Nation, Governance and Modernity in China* (Stanford, CA: Stanford University Press, 2000), and Michael G. Murdock, *Disarming the Allies of Imperialism: The State, Agitation, and Manipulation during China's Nationalist Revolution, 1922–1929* (Ithaca, NY: E. Asia Program, Cornell University, 2006). Other information I present in the Preface regarding Sun and modern China is general and widely available.

Cover Page

The front piece quotation from Ibn Khaldun is taken from his *The Muqaddimah: An Introduction to History*, trans. Franz Rosenthal, ed. N. J. Dawood (Princeton, NJ: Princeton University Press, 1967), p. 30.

Chapter 1

I begin the chapter with a discussion of Sun's 1894 letter to Qing administrator Li Hongzhang. While the biographical information regarding Sun at this time derives from Schiffrin's *Origins*, ch. 2, the quotations from Sun's letter to Li come from the translation of the letter provided in Julie Lee Wei et al., eds.,

Prescriptions for Saving China: Selected Writings of Sun Yat-sen (Stanford, CA: Hoover Institute Press, 1994): "their people can fully employ . . ." (4), "ignoring the root . . ." (4), "the skies are full of storms . . ." (11), and "In the West . . ." (11). Information appearing in later sections of Chapter 1 is widely available and is provided as a service to world history students unfamiliar with China.

Chapter 2

Much of the information on Sun's childhood and his life as a teenager in Hawaii comes from Schiffrin's *Origins*, chs. 2 and 3. My description of the position of ethnic Chinese in nineteenth-century Hawaii draws on material in Clarence E. Glick, *Sojourners and Settlers: Chinese Migrants in Hawaii* (Honolulu, HI: University of Hawaii Press, 1980), ch. 1. The quotation from Sun's father regarding taking the "Jesus nonsense" out of Sun appears in Sidney H. Chang and Leonard H. D. Gordon, *All Under Heaven: Sun Yat-sen and His Revolutionary Thought* (Stanford: Hoover Press, 1991), p. 7.

My discussion of secret societies draws on L. Eve Armentrout Ma, *Revolutionaries, Monarchists, and Chinatowns: Chinese Politics in the Americas and the 1911 Revolution* (Honolulu, HI: University of Hawaii Press, 1990), ch. 1. The material on the significance of Hong Kong derives from Jan Morris, *Hong Kong: Epilogue to an Empire* (New York: Vintage, 1985). My description of Sun as a medical doctor includes information from both Schiffrin, *Origins*, ch. 2, and Kan-Wen Ma, "Sun Yat-sen (1866–1925), A Man to Cure Patients and the Nation—His Early Years and Medical Career" (*Journal of Medical Biography*, vol. 4, no. 3, 1996), 161–170.

The bulk of my description of the Self-Strengthening Movement is based on widely available information. However, it includes material on the Empress Dowager Cixi from Jonathan D. Spence, *The Search for Modern China*, 2nd ed. (New York: Norton, 1999), ch. 10, and a quotation from Immanuel C. Y. Hsü, *The Rise of Modern China*, 5th ed. (New York: Oxford University Press, 1995), p. 262. The quotation from Sun regarding the Sino-French war appears in Leonard Shih-lien Hsü, trans., *Sun Yat-sen: His Political and Social Ideals* (Los Angeles: University of Southern California Press, 1933), p. 46. The reference to Sun's positive impression of Chinese dockworkers who refused to service a French vessel during the war draws on Schiffrin, *Origins*, pp. 18–19. More generally, much of the material regarding Sun's political activities during his period at medical school derives from Schiffrin's *Origins*, ch. 2. However, the Sun quotation regarding Darwin et al. is taken from James Reeve Pusey's *China and Charles Darwin* (Cambridge: Council on East Asian Studies, Harvard University Press, 1983), p. 318. The quotation from Sun's letter to Li Hongzhang comes from Julie Lee Wei et al., eds., *Prescriptions for Saving China*, p. 5.

Much of my discussion of the Revive China Society draws on Schiffrin's *Origins*, ch. 3, and the quotation of the oath used by the Hong Kong branch of the Society appears on page 49 of that source. Within my discussion of the 1895

Guangzhou Uprising, the reference to the description of Sun in a Singapore newspaper as a traditional Chinese bandit chief comes from Yen Ching-Hwang, *The Ethnic Chinese in East and Southeast Asia: Business, Culture and Politics* (Singapore: Times Academic Press, 2002), p. 351.

Chapter 3

The prefatory information for the London kidnapping draws on such sources as Schiffrin's *Origins*, ch. 5, Bergère's *Sun Yat-sen*, ch. 2, and Chang and Gordon's *All Under Heaven*, ch. 2. The quotations from Sun regarding the kidnapping itself—"I was gradually . . ." and "You are now in China"— appear in his *Kidnapped in London*, pages 35 and 37, respectively. However, the quote regarding his likely torture is taken from Chang and Gordon's *All Under Heaven*, p. 24. As background to my analysis of Sun's depiction of the event, I consulted John Y. Wong, *The Origins of an Heroic Image: Sun Yat-sen in London, 1896–1897* (Hong Kong: Oxford University Press, 1986). The quotation labeling Sun an "egoistic Christian" for his response to the event appears in Bergère's *Sun Yat-sen*, p. 6. My description of the early Kang Youwei draws heavily on Jonathan D. Spence, *The Gate of Heavenly Peace: The Chinese and Their Revolution, 1895–1980* (New York: Penguin, 1981), ch. 1.

Chapter 4

In my description of Chinese responses to the Boxer Uprising, the phrase "sliced up like a melon" is a translation of the frequently repeated Chinese term, *guafen*. As the chapter proceeds, I draw on material from Marius B. Jansen, *The Japanese and Sun Yat-sen* (Cambridge: Harvard University Press, 1954) at various points. That includes several quotations (all but the first two from Sun himself): "Know the shame . . ." (75), "Since Japan had freed herself . . ." (8), "That rotten Confucianist . . ." (80), "Japan today has become acquainted . . ." (211), "If there were Europeans here tonight . . ." (160), "the watchman of Asia" (120), and "We are the 'men of determination' . . ." (219). I also draw on Jansen's book with my reference to Sun's use of the "rich country, strong military" formula in his letter to Li Hongzhang (61) and my invocation of Jansen's view that Japanese officials would turn to Sun when they lacked other options (10, 105). In the section on the Huizhou Uprising, the quotation of Sun comes from his *Memoirs of a Chinese Revolutionary*, p. 198.

My quotations from Miyazaki Tôten regarding his first encounter with Sun are all taken from Miyazaki Tôten, *My Thirty-Three Years' Dream: The Autobiography of Miyazaki Tôten* (Princeton, NJ: Princeton University Press, 1982). In order of appearance, these are as follows: "He had not rinsed . . ." (133), "take power over . . ." (133), "became more and more impassioned . . ." (134), and "How noble his thought . . ." (137–8). I quote from Schiffrin's *Origins*—"there was a unique warmth . . ." (145)—near the end of the chapter.

Chapter 5

The section on Chinese students in early twentieth-century Japan draws on Marius B. Jansen, *Japan and China: From War to Peace, 1894–1972* (Chicago, IL: Rand McNally, 1975), ch. 5, along with Ranbir Vohra, *China's Path to Modernization: A Historical Review from 1800 to the Present* (Upper Saddle River, NJ: Prentice Hall, 1987), ch. 4. The discussion of Liang Qichao is influenced by Hao Chang, *Liang Ch'i-ch'ao and Intellectual Transition in China, 1890–1907* (Cambridge: Harvard University Press, 1971), ch. 6. The Liang quotation "We must have ten thousand eyes . . ." appears in John E. Wills, Jr., *Mountain of Fame: Portraits in Chinese History* (Princeton, NJ: Princeton University Press, 1994), pp. 280–1. The recapitulation of Sun's locomotive analogy utilizes material in James Reeve Pusey's *China and Charles Darwin*, pp. 341–2. The quotations from Zou Rong appear in Tsou Jung, *The Revolutionary Army: A Nationalist Tract of 1903* (The Hague-Paris: Mouton & Co., 1968), pp. 58, 109. The Sun quotation regarding the end of the Russo-Japanese War appears in the English translation of his 1924 Kobe speech as given in T'ang Leang-Li, ed., *China and Japan: Natural Friends, Unnatural Enemies* (Shanghai: China United Press, 1941), p. 143. The discussion of the creation of the Revolutionary Alliance draws on Schiffrin, *Origins*, ch. 12.

Chapter 6

The references to Sun's comparisons between his Three People's Principles and the slogans of Abraham Lincoln and the French Revolution, respectively, are drawn from Chang and Gordon's *All Under Heaven*, ch. 5. Many of the Sun quotations in this chapter—including all of those in the sections on the first two people's principles—come from Sun's *San Min Chu I*: "What is a principle? . . ." (1), "we are being crushed . . ." (10), "the more will subjugate . . ." (6), "when two Chinese meet . . ." (31), "If we take the clans . . ." (31), "a sheet of loose sand" (2, passim), "must break down individual liberty . . ." (75), "wronged races" (25), "although their government was autocratic . . ." (58), "people's rights" (58), "opposition to government" (114), "When we have a real republic . . ." (65), "the great majority . . ." (119–20), "The nation is a great automobile . . ." (126), and "the most complete . . ." (148).

The quotation from Bergère regarding Sun's future "world of justice" appears in her *Sun Yat-sen*, p. 369, as does Sun's invocation of a future "great harmony" (*datong*). The discussion of Henry George draws on ch. 5 of that work, as well as assorted readings on George, particularly a helpful entry on him in *American National Biography*, vol. 8 (New York: Oxford University Press, 1999). The quotation from David Strand appears in his "Community, Society and History in Sun Yat-sen's *Sanmin Zhuyi*," located in Theodor Huters et al., eds., *Culture and State in Chinese History: Conventions, Accommodations, and Critiques* (Stanford, CA: Stanford University Press, 1997), p. 345. Sun's statement that all Chinese including the seemingly rich are actually poor appears in *San Min Chu I*, p. 172, while his recommendation that capitalism be used to create socialism in China appears in *The International Development of China*, p. 298. John King Fairbank's assessment of Sun's writings appears in his *The Great Chinese Revolution 1800–1985* (New York: Harper & Row, 1986), p. 147.

Chapter 7

The discussion of Crane Brinton's *The Anatomy of Revolution* draws on my reading of that work, especially ch. 9. The Tocqueville quotation that ends that section appears in Alexis de Tocqueville, *The Old Regime and the Revolution*, vol. 1 (Chicago, IL: University of Chicago Press, 1998), p. 222. My overview of the conflicts between reformists and revolutionaries draws on Schiffrin's *Origins*, ch. 11; I substituted "emperor-protection" for "*bao-huang*" in Schiffrin's translation of Sun's assessment of Liang Qichao as it appears in *Origins*, p. 321. The quotations from Sun's "The True Solution of the Chinese Problem" appear in the original English in Zhongguo Guomindang dangshi weiyuanhui [The Chinese Nationalist Party Committee of Party History], ed., *Guofu Quanji* [Complete Works of the Father of the Nation], vol. 5, pages 119 and 121, respectively. The Bergère quotation regarding Sun's view of institutions is taken from her *Sun Yat-sen*, p. 142. The Sun quotation that calls overseas Chinese the "mother of the revolution" appears in Chang and Gordon's *All Under Heaven*, p. 18.

My discussion of Sun's activities in France was greatly aided by Jeffrey G. Barlow, *Sun Yat-sen and the French, 1900–1908* (U.C. Berkeley Institute of East Asian Studies, 1979). Much of the information on Yuan Shikai's early career derives from the entry on him in Howard L. Boorman, ed., *Biographical Dictionary of Republican China* (New York: Columbia University Press, 1967–1979). Likewise, the entry in that dictionary on Huang Xing was useful in my presentation of him in the chapter. For the downturn in the Emperor Protection Society's fortunes, I turned to Spence's *The Gate of Heavenly Peace*, ch. 3. The material on Homer Lea draws on several sources, foremost among them Bergère, *Sun Yat-sen*, ch. 6.

Chapter 8

My description of the Guangzhou Uprising of 1911 draws on Bergère's *Sun Yat-sen*, ch. 6. The discussion of the Railway Protection Movement includes information from Spence's *The Search for Modern China*, ch. 11. The depiction of the Wuchang Uprising draws on Vohra's *China's Path to Modernization*, ch. 4, with the anecdote about Li Yuanhong being offered the position of "George Washington of China" appearing on page 102 of that source. Other sources for the section include Hsü's *The Rise of Modern China*, ch. 20, and the entry in Boorman's *Biographical Dictionary of Republican China* on Yuan Shikai. My description of Sun's whereabouts during the revolution draws on material from C. Martin Wilbur's classic biography, *Sun Yat-sen: Frustrated Patriot* (New York: Columbia University Press, 1976), ch. 3.

The quotation from Sun's telegram to Yuan on January 1, 1912, is taken from Li Chien-Nung, *The Political History of China, 1840–1928* (Princeton, NJ: D. Van Nostrand Co., 1956), p. 260. My description of Sun's short period as provisional president of China utilizes material from Bergère's *Sun Yat-sen*, ch. 7. My presentation of Sun's deal to transfer power to Yuan Shikai draws on Hsü's *The Rise of Modern China*, ch. 20. My assessment of the 1911 revolution draws heavily on James E. Sheridan, *China in Disintegration: The Republican Era in Chinese History, 1912–1949* (New York: Free Press, 1975), ch. 2, and my Sheridan quotation is taken from page 55 of this work.

Chapter 9

The material on Sun's view of railways derives from several sources. Chang and Gordon's *All Under Heaven*, ch. 3, stresses the significance of Sun's period as director of railways, with page 51 providing the Sun quotation that links national wealth to rail mileage. The quotation from Sun's letter to Li Hongzhang appears in Julie Lee Wei et al., eds., *Prescriptions for Saving China*, p. 12. Chang Jui-Te, "Technology Transfer in Modern China: The Case of Railway Enterprise (1876–1937)," *Modern Asian Studies* (vol. 27, no. 2, 1993) and Richard Louis Edmonds, "The Legacy of Sun Yat-sen's Railway Plans," *China Quarterly* (vol. 111, September 1987) each contain helpful general information on railroads in early twentieth-century China. Meanwhile, Arthur Rosenbaum, "Railway Enterprise and Economic Development: The Case of the Imperial Railways of North China, 1900–1911," *Modern China* (vol. 2, no. 2, April 1976), provides a sobering view of the obstacles China faced in developing a unified, profitable rail network.

The John King Fairbank quotation on the assassination of Song Jiaoren is taken from his *The United States and China*, 4th ed. (Cambridge: Harvard University Press, 1976), p. 222. The description of Sun's link to the Japanese government at the time of the attempted Second Revolution draws on material in Jansen's *The Japanese and Sun Yat-sen*, ch. 7. Sun's characterization of China as a "potential India" for Japan is introduced on page 189 of this source. The Sun quotation from the occasion of his creation of the Chinese Revolutionary Party appears in Bergère's *Sun Yat-sen*, p. 257. The description of Sun's response to the Japanese government's Twenty-One Demands utilizes information from Jansen's *The Japanese and Sun Yat-sen*, ch. 8. The Schiffrin quotation on Sun's ability to return from defeat appears in his *Origins*, p. 2. Near the end of the chapter, the material on the warlord era draws on several sources, foremost among them Sheridan's *China in Disintegration*, ch. 3.

Chapter 10

The quotation from C. Martin Wilbur in the first paragraph of the chapter appears in his *Sun Yat-sen*, p. 38. The story about Sun's favorite "things" appears in Li Ao, *Sun Zhongshan yanjiu* [A Study of Sun Yatsen] (Taipei: Li Ao chubanshe,

1987), p. 285. In addition to scattered passages in Schiffrin's *Origins* and Bergère's *Sun Yat-sen*, a major source on which I drew for information regarding Sun's various relationships was *The Relatives and Descendants of Dr. Sun Yat-sen* (Beijing: Encyclopedia of China Publishing House, 2001), a bilingual photo album compiled by the staff of the Museum of Dr. Sun Yat-sen in Cuiheng, PRC. This source, page 4, supplied my reference to Sun's followers calling Lu Muzhen "Grand Madame Sun" and "Grand Madame Lu." Some of the information regarding Lu Muzhen's later years comes from Lyon Sharmon, *Sun Yat-sen: His Life and its Meaning* (New York: John Day, 1934), ch. 6, a seminal biography. The material on Sun's marriage to Ôtsuki Kaori derives from Li Ao's *Sun Zhongshan yanjiu*, pp. 293–6, which introduces Kubota Bunji's research on the subject. The quotation from Sun's daughter Miyakawa Fumiko is my translation of a Chinese rendition that appears on page 296 of that source.

The description of the young Charlie Soong draws on Sterling Seagrave, *The Soong Dynasty* (New York: Harper & Row, 1985), ch. 2, while the description of the young Soong Qingling utilizes that volume's ch. 6. For the adult Qingling, a very helpful source was Jung Chang and Jon Halliday, *Madame Sun Yat-sen* (New York: Penguin, 1986), especially chs. 1 and 2. I utilized three quotations of Qingling from that book: "It was a romantic girl's idea . . ." (30–1), "He made it all up . . ." (38), and "The fact that I was loyal . . ." (34). Seagrave's *The Soong Dynasty*, ch. 11, provided useful information regarding Qingling's break with Chiang Kaishek; its page 238 supplied my reference to certain American journalists at the time characterizing Qingling as China's "Joan of Arc." My reference to Qingling's positive assessment of Stalin is based on her remarks in "For Stalin's Birthday," a short essay that appears in Soong Ching Ling, *The Struggle for New China* (Peking: Foreign Languages Press, 1953), pp. 226–7.

Chapter 11

My description of China in World War I draws on several sources, including Spence's *The Search for Modern China*, ch. 12 and Wilbur's *Sun Yat-sen*, ch. 4. My characterization of the contents of Sun's telegram to David Lloyd George derives from page 92 of Wilbur's *Sun Yat-sen*, while the slightly later discussion of Sun's links with German government agents is based on pages 93–4. The two quotations from Sun's interview with a Japanese reporter are taken from K. K. Kawakami, "Sun Yat-sen's Greater Asia Doctrine," *Contemporary Japan, a Review of Japanese Affairs* (vol. 4, no. 2, September 1935), 242. The discussion of Sun's creation of his first Guangzhou government draws further on Wilbur's *Sun Yat-sen*, ch. 4. My reference to Sun giving Chen Jiongming an army and a base in Fujian is based on the entry on Chen in Wang Ke-Wen, ed., *Modern China: An Encyclopedia of History, Culture, and Nationalism* (New York: Garland, 1998), a volume I found useful in other contexts as well.

J. A. G. Roberts, *Modern China: An Illustrated History* (Stroud, UK: Sutton Publishing, 1988), ch. 8, provided basic background on the May Fourth Movement. For Sun's response to the movement, I turned primarily to two sources: Chang and Gordon's *All Under Heaven*, ch. 3, and Y. C. Wang, *Chinese Intellectuals and the*

West 1872–1949 (Chapel Hill, NC: University of North Carolina Press, 1966), ch. 10. The quotation beginning "They really do not know . . ." appears in Chang and Gordon, p. 84. The other Sun quotations on the topic are taken from Wang: "should be excused" (334), "The achievements are bound to be . . ." (334), and "The liberty which Westerners . . ." (334–5), respectively.

The quotations from Sun's *The International Development of China* appear in the translation introduced at the beginning of this Note: "dumping ground" (3), "New World . . ." (8), "become two continuous cities" (71), "the rapids should be dammed . . ." (92), and "our labouring class . . ." (296). The same applies to the quotations from Sun's *Memoirs of a Chinese Revolutionary*: "Actions are difficult . . ." (7), "knowledge is difficult . . ." (57), "In order to become . . ." (114), and "just as easy . . . " (11). The quotation from Mao Zedong is taken from his "The Great Union of Popular Masses" (translated in *China Quarterly*, vol. 49, January–March 1972), 79.

Chapter 12

The quotation from Ming K. Chan regarding Guangzhou in the early 1920s appears in his "A Turning Point in the Modern Chinese Revolution: The Historical Significance of the Canton Decade, 1917–1927," in Gail Hershatter et al., eds., *Remapping China: Fissures in Historical Terrain* (Stanford, CA: Stanford University Press, 1996), p. 225. The discussion regarding Chen Jiongming draws on an academic work by his daughter, Leslie H. Dingyan Chen. This work, *Chen Jiongming and the Federalist Movement: Regional Leadership and Nation Building in Early Republican China* (Ann Arbor, MI: University of Michigan Center for Chinese Studies, 1999), is a fascinating, fastidious, and sometimes tendentious account of Chen's interactions with Sun during the latter's second Guangzhou government. The two Sun quotations in the section on the Chen–Sun showdown are taken from *Chen Jiongming and the Federalist Movement*, pages 183 and 191, respectively. The excerpted quotation from Soong Qingling on the military action against Sun appears in a fuller form in Seagrave's *The Soong Dynasty*, pp. 168–9.

Regarding Lenin's view of Asia, the translation of his "Theses on the National and Colonial Questions" in Robert C. Tucker, ed., *The Lenin Anthology* (New York: W. W. Norton, 1975) was useful. Lenin's reference to anticolonial activities as a "flank attack" on Western capitalism appears in John King Fairbank's *The United States and China*, p. 237. Lenin's remark that "[t]he East will help us to conquer the West" is taken from Peter Hopkirk, *Setting the East Ablaze: Lenin's Dream of an Empire in Asia* (Oxford: Oxford University Press, 1986), p. 1. One source I consulted for the context of Sun's alliance with the U.S.S.R. was Dan N. Jacobs, "Soviet Russia and Chinese Nationalism in the 1920s," in F. Gilbert Chan et al., eds., *China in the 1920s: Nationalism and Revolution* (New York: New Viewpoints, 1976). My reference to Sun's bodyguards and "two-gun" Cohen in particular draws on Daniel Levy, *Two-Gun Cohen: A Biography* (New York: St. Martin's, 1997). For information on Borodin, I turned to the fascinating chapter on him in Jonathan D. Spence, *To Change China: Western Advisers in China*

1620–1960 (New York: Viking Penguin, 1980). Sun's descriptions of Borodin as his "Lafayette" and Lenin as "exceptional" appear in Bergère's *Sun Yat-sen*, pages 315 and 325, respectively. Sun's remarks on Marxism are taken from the first essay on people's livelihood in his *San Min Chu I*: "Class war is not . . ." (161), "Marx can only be called . . ." (161), "the facts of Western history . . ." (164), and "Marx said that . . ." (165–6).

The reference to "Red Canton" appears in various sources, including Chang and Halliday's *Madame Sun*, p. 47. The Sun biographer who characterized the Sun of the 1910s as "crossing the desert" is Bergère in her *Sun Yat-sen*, p. 246. The three Sun quotations on the Soviet Union all appear in Wilbur's *Sun Yat-sen*: "We no longer look . . ." (189), "I do not care what . . ." (146), and "We may merely yoke up . . ." (175).

Chapter 13

The term "Asiatics" used by Sun in his pan-Asianism speech appears in T'ang Leang-Li, ed., *China and Japan*, p. 150. The quotation from the Leader's Will follows the translation given in Wilbur's *Sun Yat-sen*, p. 278. The Seagrave quotation appears in his *The Soong Dynasty*, p. 201. The phrase "peace, struggle, save China" is employed at the exhibit at the Museum of Dr. Sun Yat-sen, Cuiheng, PRC.

The quotations from the eulogy at the Christian service for Sun all appear in Seagrave's *The Soong Dynasty*, p. 203. The description of Sun's burial at the Azure Cloud Temple draws on Sharmon's *Sun Yat-sen*, ch. 9. The description of the reburial in Nanjing utilizes "Teakwood Funeral Coach" from *Time* magazine (vol. 13, no. 22, June 3, 1929), 29. The description of the reading of the Leader's Will in GMD-led China derives from Sharmon's *Sun Yat-sen*, ch. 10. The contrast between Sun's admiration for Hong Xiuquan and Chiang Kaishek's admiration for Zeng Guofan is analyzed in Mary C. Wright, ed., "From Revolution to Restoration: The Transformation of Kuomintang Ideology," in Joseph R. Levenson, ed., *Modern China: An Interpretive Anthology* (London: Macmillan, 1971). The discussion of Wang Jingwei draws on the entry on him in Boorman's *Biographical Dictionary of Republican China*. The invocation of Mary Matossian refers to her essay "Ideologies of Delayed Industrialization: Some Tensions and Ambiguities," which forms ch. 6 of John H. Kautsky, ed., *Political Change in Underdeveloped Countries: Nationalism and Communism* (New York: John Wiley and Sons, 1967).

Index